D0219948

The Yugoslav Wars of the 1990s

Studies in European History Series

Series Editors:	Sarah Badcock
	Julian Jackson
	Peter Wilson

Studies in European History
Series Standing Order ISBN 978–0-333–79365–7
(outside North America only)

You can receive future titles in this series as they are published by placing a standing order. Please contact your bookseller or, in case of difficulty, write to us at the address below with your name and address, the title of the series and the ISBN quoted above.

Customer Services Department, Macmillan Distribution Ltd,
Houndmills, Basingstoke, Hampshire, RG21 6XS, UK

The Yugoslav Wars
of the 1990s

Catherine Baker

 palgrave

© Catherine Baker 2015

All rights reserved. No reproduction, copy or transmission of this publication may be made without written permission.

No portion of this publication may be reproduced, copied or transmitted save with written permission or in accordance with the provisions of the Copyright, Designs and Patents Act 1988, or under the terms of any licence permitting limited copying issued by the Copyright Licensing Agency, Saffron House, 6–10 Kirby Street, London EC1N 8TS.

Any person who does any unauthorized act in relation to this publication may be liable to criminal prosecution and civil claims for damages.

The author has asserted her right to be identified as the author of this work in accordance with the Copyright, Designs and Patents Act 1988.

First published 2015 by
PALGRAVE

Palgrave in the UK is an imprint of Macmillan Publishers Limited, registered in England, company number 785998, of 4 Crinan Street, London, N1 9XW.

Palgrave Macmillan in the US is a division of St Martin's Press LLC, 175 Fifth Avenue, New York, NY 10010.

Palgrave is a global imprint of the above companies and is represented throughout the world.

Palgrave® and Macmillan® are registered trademarks in the United States, the United Kingdom, Europe and other countries.

ISBN 978–1–137–39898–7

This book is printed on paper suitable for recycling and made from fully managed and sustained forest sources. Logging, pulping and manufacturing processes are expected to conform to the environmental regulations of the country of origin.

A catalogue record for this book is available from the British Library.

A catalog record for this book is available from the Library of Congress.

Typeset by MPS Limited, Chennai, India.

Printed in China

Contents

Contents

Editors' Preface

The Studies in European History series offers a guide to developments in a field of history that has become increasingly specialized with the sheer volume of new research and literature now produced.

Each book has three main objectives. The primary purpose is to offer an informed assessment of opinion on a key episode or theme in European history. Secondly, each title presents a distinct interpretation and conclusions from someone who is closely involved with current debates in the field. Thirdly, it provides students and teachers with a succinct introduction to the topic, with the essential information necessary to understand it and the literature being discussed. Equipped with an annotated bibliography and other aids to study, each book provides an ideal starting point from which to explore important events and processes that have shaped Europe's history to the present day.

Books in the series introduce students to historical approaches which, in some cases, are very new and which, in the normal course of things, would take many years to filter down to textbooks. By presenting history's cutting edge, we hope that the series will demonstrate some of the excitement that historians, like scientists, feel as they work on the frontiers of their subjects. The series also has an important contribution to make in publicizing what historians are doing, and making it accessible to students and scholars in this and related disciplines.

Sarah Badcock
Julian Jackson
Peter H. Wilson

Acknowledgements

I could not have completed this book without the support and understanding of my colleagues in History at the University of Hull. Staff at the Brynmor Jones Library, the UCL School of Slavonic and East European Studies Library and the British Library kindly assisted the bibliographic research. Thanks are due to all those who volunteered their time to comment on drafts of the manuscript or update me about forthcoming work (including Rory Archer, Wendy Bracewell, Dejan Djokić, Eric Gordy, Laura McLeod, Dragana Obradović, Jelena Obradović-Wochnik, Ljubica Spaskovska and Jamie Steels) but none bear any responsibility for the compromises I have had to make in representing this contested field within a restricted space. My deepest thanks go to the students I have taught at Hull, SSEES and the University of Southampton, especially the Hull students in 2013–14 whose Yugoslavia module coincided with my writing this book: their experiences in studying this aspect of the recent past have all shaped how I review interpretations of it today.

List of Abbreviations

ARBiH	Army of the Republic of Bosnia-Herzegovina
ARK	Autonomous Region of Krajina
AVNOJ	Anti-Fascist Council of the People's Liberation of Yugoslavia
BiH	Bosnia-Herzegovina
EC	European Community
EU	European Union
FRY	Federal Republic of Yugoslavia
FYROM	Former Yugoslav Republic of Macedonia
HDZ	Croatian Democratic Union
HOS	Croatian Defence Forces
HSP	Croatian Party of Right
HVO	Croat Defence Council
ICJ	International Court of Justice
ICTY	International Criminal Tribunal for the Former Yugoslavia
IFOR	Implementation Force
IMF	International Monetary Fund
JCE	Joint Criminal Enterprise
JNA	Yugoslav People's Army
KFOR	Kosovo Force
KLA	Kosovo Liberation Army
KPJ	Communist Party of Yugoslavia
LDK	Democratic League of Kosovo
NATO	North Atlantic Treaty Organization
NDH	Independent State of Croatia

NLA	National Liberation Army
OHR	Office of the High Representative
OTP	Office of the Prosecutor
RDC	Research and Documentation Centre
RS	Republika Srpska
RSK	Republic of Serb Krajina
SANU	Serbian Academy of Sciences and Arts
SAO	Serb Autonomous Region
SDA	Party of Democratic Action
SDP	Party of Democratic Change
SDS	Serb Democratic Party
SKJ	League of Communists of Yugoslavia
SNSD	Alliance of Independent Social Democrats
SPS	Socialist Party of Serbia
SRS	Serbian Radical Party
SRSJ	Association of Reformist Forces of Yugoslavia
TO	Territorial Defence
TRC	Truth and Reconciliation Commission
UJDI	Association for a Yugoslav Democratic Initiative
UNHCR	United Nations High Commissioner for Refugees
UNMIK	United Nations Mission in Kosovo
UNMOP	United Nations Mission of Observers in Prevlaka
UNPROFOR	United Nations Protection Force
UNSC	United Nations Security Council
UNTAES	United Nations Transitional Administration in Eastern Slavonia
VJ	Army of Yugoslavia
VMRO	Internal Macedonian Revolutionary Organization
VRS	Army of Republika Srpska
ZNG	(in Croatia) National Guard

Introduction

The Yugoslav wars involved the violent destruction of a society of 23 million people that was simultaneously undergoing the consequences of the collapse of Yugoslav socialism. Between 1991 and 1999, the wars in Slovenia, Croatia, Bosnia-Herzegovina and Kosovo caused the death of approximately 140,000 people, 100,000 in Bosnia-Herzegovina. If the wars include the smaller-scale 2001 Macedonian conflict, they could even be said to have lasted into the 2000s. The Yugoslav wars were Europe's most serious security crisis since the early Cold War, and led to the first international war crimes tribunal since the Nuremberg and Tokyo trials. They also made the ex-Yugoslav region, especially Bosnia-Herzegovina and Kosovo, a test-bed for a new post-conflict peacebuilding model. Meanwhile, the development of scholarly literature on the wars exemplified the problems and politics of researching, understanding and narrating the recent past.

This book gives an introductory account of English-language literature on the Yugoslav wars, aiming to suggest what debates readers should be aware of if they (as they should) read further. Although many facts about the wars can and should be firmly established, scholarly interpretations of them diverge widely. Some disputes can be resolved with newly-available evidence; others involve differing approaches to the ethics and philosophy of history and cannot be so easily reconciled. This book tries to give some sense of what these controversies put at stake and to suggest some important dimensions which are still under-researched. It will also prompt readers to think about their own ethical commitments, which ultimately affect how anyone interprets the wars. A fair number of publications on the Yugoslav wars have assessed the contemporaneous state of the field [see the 'Historiography' section of the Bibliography], but were mostly conversations among specialists, whereas previous introductory texts [6; 13] were not centred on these debates. This book bridges that gap, taking as its source materials the published works.

The clearest scholarly arguments to identify concern the course of events themselves. First and foremost is simply 'Who was responsible?', and indeed many scholars view accounts as incomplete if they do not answer the responsibility question. Secondly is how far Yugoslavia's structural instabilities as a state and society contributed to its break-up. This structural question does not necessarily preclude assessing responsibility, even if some structurally-focused works underplay responsibility too far. The instability problem itself has long-term and short-term dimensions: did the flaws appear during Communist Yugoslavia, during the Second World War, during Yugoslav unification in 1918, or even before? And, lastly, how far could foreign governments and international organizations, especially Western powers, be said to have exacerbated the wars? The literature contains arguments about what to write, but also *how* to write about the conflicts.

During these debates, certain words have come to communicate wider messages. Writing of 'aggression' – especially the aggression of Slobodan Milošević and the Yugoslav People's Army (JNA) against Slovenia, Croatia and Bosnia-Herzegovina – conveys a different view to writing solely of a 'civil war' [215: 51–3]. Using or not using the word 'genocide', and how broadly, will often also be read as a signal about an overall interpretation of the wars, so these decisions are not value-neutral. Beyond the politics of these symbolic words, terminological issues arise in almost every sentence: for instance, how far can one describe actions as being taken by a national group, which saves words but implies that nations act homogenously? Writing that 'the Croats' (or 'the Serbs' or 'the Bosniaks') launched an offensive, compared to writing that the Croat Defence Council (or the Army of Republika Srpska, or the Army of the Republic of Bosnia-Herzegovina) did so, conveys different impressions about who conflicts are really 'between' [35; 405].

Different understandings of nationalism and ethnicity also affect interpretations of the wars. During the 1990s, scholars writing in English often tried to challenge a prevailing popular view of the Yugoslav wars as a conflict between opposing ethnic groups based on long-term grievances and fears. Instead, they emphasized proximate political and military causes [46]. Both positions still tended to view ethnic groups and nations as relatively fixed, stable entities. Simultaneously, however, some social scientists' reinterpretations of ethnicity and nationalism would influence future research on the Yugoslav wars (and earlier periods). Viewing organizations (such as political parties or militaries), rather than ethnic or national groups, as the real protagonists of ethnic conflict – and arguing that these organizations gained ideological power by successfully claiming to represent the whole of a nation – complicated the link between ethnicity and war [154]. This 'constructivist' view broke down (or 'deconstructed') common-sense understandings about ethnic groups and ethnic conflicts, and some scholars of the Yugoslav wars used this idea to argue that too much emphasis on the conflicts' ethnic dimension took attention away from the struggles for political and military power *within* every group that was involved [14]. It is hard to express this analysis without attributing actions to organizations, institutions and individuals instead of ethno-national groups, even though it lengthens sentences.

How to think about the nation had, by the early 2000s, become the most important question in south-east European studies. Nationalism – the political principle that nations exist and that nationhood grants people the right to political self-determination over a defined national territory – made the idea of a Yugoslav state possible, but also underlay the self-determination movements that competed with it. Ethnicity – the idea of groups of humans with their own distinct cultures and 'homelands' who believe they share a common history and common lines of descent – is not always the basis for claims to be recognized as nations, though in the Yugoslav area almost always was. With nationalism and ethnicity being so important to understand, the literature contains dozens of examples of what Wendy Bracewell called 'history in the national mode', that is, recounting the past of a particular country, region or national group and offering this as a long-term explanation for the 1990s [41: 150]. Bracewell's next observation is also worth amplifying: that '[t]he nation persists as a taken-for-granted category of analysis [...], often without critical attention to the assumptions that underpin it' [41: 150]. Such critical attention may mean asking different research questions.

Hugh Poulton, for instance, titled a survey of Macedonian history *Who Are The Macedonians?* [302], whereas another scholar of contemporary Macedonia, Keith Brown, would rather not even ask that question. Brown's questions were about the various ways of imagining who Macedonians were (and who was not Macedonian) [296: 20–1]. Some specialist works take their destabilization of 'national identity' as far as refusing to use modern-day national labels for earlier periods, to reinforce their argument that these identities were actively created in the 19th or even 20th centuries [60; 68]. But the argument also has live consequences for narrating the recent past. Recent academic research has often deconstructed the foundations of ideas about nationalism and ethnicity more than some readers may be used to (depending on what they may have read about nationalism before). One major problem in this book is how far questions about nationalism and ethnicity can explain the Yugoslav wars. Another, which it would be irresponsible for an introductory text to avoid, is that of guilt and responsibility.

Some researchers see assessing responsibility as their primary task. Prosecutors at the International Criminal Tribunal for the Former Yugoslavia (ICTY) certainly had to, but some academic researchers also held that their primary task was documenting objective truth about the wars. Sabrina Ramet, for instance, extensively states what she terms a 'moral universalist' position [53: 1–27]. This rejects as postmodern any attempt to question whether objective truths exist or to reduce history to the study of narratives only: from a universalist perspective, these intellectual exercises led to relativistic suggestions that guilt lay on all sides [52; 159]. The dispute began in the mid-1990s but still echoes through some more recent works: a 2014 book by Edina Bećirević, for instance, criticized a 'fashionable post-modern concept' for giving 'the same voice to victims and perpetrators' about the Bosnian war [206: xii].

While some debates have continued since the 1990s, other directions in the literature are new. The vast amount of documents released by the ICTY has started facilitating a new archival turn. Anthropologists meanwhile led a turn towards local, microhistorical studies of the conflicts, covering post-war reconstruction and reconciliation as well as wartime events. These microhistories opened questions about the wars' socio-economic dimensions and reminded scholars that the Yugoslav successor states were post-conflict *and* post-socialist societies [318]: the

4

same dislocations that affected eastern Europe and the former USSR after Communism collapsed also played out in former Yugoslavia, but intersected there with dynamics of armed conflict. Incorporating new perspectives into the core history of the wars, the structure of this book introduces the main debates as the English language literature currently stands.

Chapter 1, covering long-term history, explains competing narratives about the Yugoslav region's past that circulated before, during and after the 1990s. The short-term background of 1980s Yugoslavia's multiple crises is discussed in Chapter 2, on explanations for the break-up of the Yugoslav federation. Chapter 3, on 1990–91 and the Slovenian and Croatian wars of independence, explains why the break-up of Yugoslavia was violent (including assessments of Milošević, the Yugoslav People's Army (JNA), the militias of the Serb Democratic Party (SDS) in Croatia, and the new Croatian president, Franjo Tuđman) and how the new states consolidated themselves. The longest of the wars, the 1992–95 conflict in Bosnia-Herzegovina, is the subject of Chapter 4, which shows that the controversies it caused continue to resonate. The wars' final phase, meanwhile, can now be seen as the 1998–99 Kosovo War, with consequences for Macedonia, Serbia and Montenegro as well as Kosovo (Chapter 5). Unlike older histories, newer works can assess the wars' consequences as well as their course. Chapter 6 thus discusses post-conflict peacebuilding and reconciliation, and Chapter 7 another activity that was supposed to create a lasting peace: the prosecution of war crimes through the ICTY and other courts, with the inherent objective for post-conflict societies to collectively 'come to terms with the past'. Chapter 8, on the wars' cultural and linguistic legacies, asks at first sight a paradoxical question: did a common Yugoslav culture survive even though Yugoslav society had been broken apart?

Many scholars of the Yugoslav wars could write a book of this kind. This particular book happens to have an author whose own research has aimed to be sceptical about the idea of homogenous national identities, interested in how narratives get constructed, and attentive to imbalances of power. At the same time, I am conscious that an introductory text must leave readers feeling they know more, rather than less, about the topic than before, especially in a context where narratives about the past have often been distorted for political ends. The book aims to question some popular assumptions about the history of the Yugoslav wars and to suggest some areas that researchers have not yet fully explored, but references the most up-to-date published research based on archival sources wherever it can. The study of the Yugoslav wars is not yet, and likely never will be, complete, but historians have access to more knowledge about this episode in Europe's recent past than ever before. The need to use this knowledge to ask the most comprehensive, searching questions remains.

1 Yugoslavia and Its Origins

Histories of the Yugoslav wars usually start with long-term background, and more of it than histories of other twentieth-century conflicts: one would rarely expect a study of the Western Front in 1914–18 to begin with the medieval Duchy of Burgundy, but explanations of the Yugoslav wars often start in that time frame or earlier. Indeed, debates about the wars incorporated the region's long-term past from the very outset. Which nations had historical precedence over which territories in south-east Europe? Were the region's cultural, social, economic and political legacies already too diverse in 1918, when the first Yugoslav state formed, for the successful unification of South Slavs into one state? Could the 1990s wars even be explained as continuations of historical inter-ethnic rivalries – or, conversely, did the past offer praiseworthy examples of tolerance and coexistence? Even scholars who reject long-term explanations as deterministic still need to explain the region's past: many statements by participants in the wars referred to specific national narratives about the past to justify present-day political and military claims. Attempting to establish which nation had first inhabited an area was a basis for establishing which nation-state it should now belong to; referring to past persecution and violence was a basis for propagating fear of persecution in the present or for putting forward moral claims that should have a bearing on present-day political control.

National claims to territory

A prerequisite for Yugoslav unification was being able to conceive of the nation, as a community bound by a shared history and a culture inherited across generations, at all. Like German or Italian

7

unification, Yugoslav unification before 1918 implied joining together territories that were then governed by several states so that the 'South Slav' nations could exercise national self-determination (the right for peoples to govern themselves on the territory they inhabit). The Yugoslav idea, however, implied several national groups exercising that right jointly. The 1918 state was described as 'the Kingdom of Serbs, Croats and Slovenes', who were all South Slavs. The second Yugoslavia, re-established by the Yugoslav Communist Party in 1943–45, eventually recognized six South Slav peoples: Serbs, Croats, Slovenes, Macedonians, Montenegrins, and eventually 'Muslims' (later also called 'Bosniaks'). Yugoslav unification implied they should exercise self-determination together rather than seeking separate national states [12].

States' and movements' claims to national sovereignty over territory rested on a link between ethnic identity (which group lived there), space (how far they extended) and time (how long they had lived there). Pursuing separate national programmes meant determining this link for each South Slav group; a Yugoslav state's external borders would need only to delineate the territory inhabited by South Slavs, though questions about internal borders and structure based on national claims to territory were still serious considerations for both Yugoslav states. However, even determining the boundaries of 'where South Slavs lived' was difficult. In the late nineteenth and early twentieth centuries, Italian, Albanian, Hungarian, Bulgarian and Greek national movements all made competing territorial claims over areas where they considered ethnic majorities favoured their own nations. Jews, Roma and Vlachs, who also lived in the region, did not have representatives seeking national states in south-east Europe at all. National territorial claims rested on interpreting demographic evidence (to show one group had a present-day majority) and historical evidence (to show one group lived there first). Interpretations of history thus became resources in political and military struggles, as did competing interpretations of present-day inhabitants' identities.

Evidence about ancient or medieval statehood was particularly valuable for nationalist movements claiming historical precedents for nation-states, on the assumption that ancient residence and sovereignty would convey present-day statehood rights. South Slavs had arrived in the region from Eurasia between the sixth and the eighth centuries AD, likely merging with existing populations rather than displacing them [70: 13–15], and their clan chiefs had become rulers within Frankish, Venetian and Byzantine spheres of influence. The medieval Croatian, Serbian and Bosnian kingdoms became future symbols of national continuity, as did Montenegrin dukes and Slovenian nobility from periods when they had flourished. Albanian narratives of national origin, meanwhile, concerned the pre-Roman period and argued the contemporary Albanian nation descended from the Illyrians who inhabited the same area during the Bronze Age. National historical narratives thus interpreted the past using nineteenth- and twentieth-century national categories. Often, these narratives clashed: for instance, when mid-twentieth-century Macedonian nationalists started incorporating ancient Macedon and Alexander the Great into their national origin narrative [302: 121], this challenged Greek national narratives where Alexander's heroism belonged to the modern Greeks. Greek and Macedonian nationalists therefore disputed the contemporary Macedonian state's right to use ancient Macedon's 'Star of Vergina' symbol or even to call itself 'Macedonia' [298].

The medieval polities, however, ended up either incorporated into larger states or split apart. The Croatian kingdom became an autonomous part of Hungary in 1102, and the Bosnian and Serbian kingdoms were both absorbed by the Ottoman Empire in 1459–63 as it expanded into south-east Europe from Anatolia. A previous battle between the armies of Sultan Murad I and Prince Lazar of Serbia at Kosovo Polje (28 June 1389), after which the Serbian kingdom became an Ottoman vassal state, became the central event in Serbian national mythology even though it was not even the most important battle in the late-fourteenth-century Ottoman campaign [124; 286]. Claims that the medieval kingdoms retained continuity rest on various grounds: the preservation of Croatia's state tradition with its own governor and assembly [70; 85]; the Serbian Orthodox Church fulfilled a continuity function for Serbs [86: 13–25; 93: 22–3]; perhaps, too, Bosnian territorial integrity (though not political autonomy) was maintained through the organization of Ottoman provinces in Bosnia-Herzegovina [74: 37; 241]. The geopolitical shift caused by the Ottoman Empire's emergence as the strongest power in south-east Europe nevertheless transformed the region's social and cultural relations [98].

Early modern south-east Europe was shaped by the conflict of Ottoman and Habsburg aspirations: Ottoman northward expansion meant conquering Habsburg lands. Between 1526 and 1791, there were seven large-scale Habsburg–Ottoman wars, plus ongoing small-scale raiding on land (especially in the Dinaric highlands) and at sea. The third power in the western Balkans, Venice, ruled most of the eastern Adriatic coast except self-governing Ragusa (now Dubrovnik) and had tense relations with both empires when Ottoman–Habsburg rivalries threatened Venetian trading interests. Imperial strategic needs and the everyday impact of warfare altered society and the economy: Ottoman or Habsburg administrative structures were re-imposed depending on who held power where, and front-line areas became depopulated as peasants left villages behind. Both empires also developed new forms of fortification and authority in border regions. In 1522, the Habsburg Empire began creating a 'Military Frontier' (Vojna Krajina), eventually placing the area from the northern Dalmatian coast to Transylvania under direct military authority. Orthodox and Catholic households displaced from south of the Frontier were readily settled there to increase Habsburg numerical strength, and in 1690–91, tens of thousands of Serbs including the head of the Church fled from Kosovo and southern Serbia into the Frontier and the region north of Belgrade [86: 6–16].

The Ottoman Empire similarly established fortified frontier districts after 1699 and militarized the local peasantry [74: 47]. However, this was a comparatively late step in the Ottoman reshaping of trade, agriculture and religion in south-east Europe. One of the earliest Ottoman policies – introducing the imperial '*millet*' system of religious autonomy – had meanwhile become the most consequential. Ottoman administrative, agrarian, economic and military systems integrated South Slav nobles, merchants and peasants who converted to the state religion, Islam, and Islam now joined Orthodox and Catholic Christianity as another religious tradition among South Slavs. The millet system gave separate religious institutions authority over Catholic, Orthodox and Muslim Slavs, and this may explain why three different ethnic and national identities (Croat, Serb and Muslim/ Bosniak) developed around these religious cores in Bosnia-Herzegovina [74: 55–6; 253: 59–64].

Two late eighteenth-/early nineteenth-century developments stimulated South Slav national movements: the weakening of Ottoman state power, and the temporary Napoleonic occupation of the Adriatic coast as the 'Illyrian Provinces' (1805/1809–15). Movements among Serbs, Bulgarians, Greeks and Romanians capitalized on the Ottoman inability to command forces in peripheral regions and launched uprisings for autonomy, as did some local elites in Egypt and what is now northern Greece/southern Albania, who had been resisting Ottoman reforms. Two Serbian uprisings in 1804–13 and 1815–30 led to Serbia being recognized as an autonomous principality. Ottoman authority over Montenegro became even weaker than before, and the secular government created by Montenegro's last 'prince-bishop', Petar II Petrović-Njegoš, drew ever closer to Russia as it sought independence from Istanbul. Napoleonic rule in the Adriatic, meanwhile, ended in 1815 when these lands were awarded to the Habsburg Empire rather than reverting to Venice. The experience was short-lived but arguably introduced the idea of popular national sovereignty into the region [68].

Nineteenth- and twentieth-century nationalist movements among South Slavs saw themselves as rediscovering or reviving their peoples' national identities. One recent historical approach, however, argues that national identities did not even exist until nineteenth-century activists and states started producing and constructing them – exemplified by the title of John Fine's book, *When Ethnicity Did Not Matter in the Balkans* [68]. Ethnic and national identities perceivable today would then have been shaped by nineteenth- and twentieth-century state structures instead [1: 212–13], demands relating to ethnic belonging and territory might be much younger than the cultural traditions they were based on, and those very traditions might have merged with each other or even been invented outright. While modern south-east European history is often interpreted as driven by clashes of national movements [15], this approach decentres the nation as a topic of inquiry and a natural political category. It seeks to re-open the question of what kinds of community people in the past considered that they belonged to [68], to refuse to tell late Ottoman history through the lens of national insurgencies [60] and to re-evaluate the Ottoman past on its own terms not today's [72].

11

Reconsidering national identification

South Slav national programmes multiplied in the mid-nineteenth century. Within the Habsburg lands, South Slavs were spread between the 'Hungarian crownlands' and several provinces in what could, after 1867 (when the Empire reorganized into the 'Dual Monarchy' of Austria–Hungary), be called the Empire's 'Austrian' half. An 'Illyrian movement' among Croats sought to unify South Slavs within the Empire. Partly responding to increasing pressure for South Slavs to assimilate into the Hungarian nation, it became a Croatian 'national revival' by the 1860s; one strand hoped all South Slavs could be unified through Croatia, while another warned that Croats would risk assimilation by Serbs if they sought unification jointly. Outside Austria–Hungary, the Kingdom of Serbia aspired to unify all Serbs, from Kosovo and Macedonia to the Habsburg lands. In 1844 the Serbian foreign minister, Ilija Garašanin, envisaged Serbia expanding to the Adriatic [1: 343–5; 2: 68–9]. Either the borders would need to incorporate the Muslim South Slavs and many Croats (though not necessarily the Slovenes), with non-Serbs as minorities, or Serbia could lead a fully 'Yugoslav' unification. Before 1900 there were thus already incompatible visions of South Slavs' political futures, complicated by competing definitions of 'Croats' and 'Serbs'. Nonetheless, Croat and Serb politicians could still sometimes co-operate within the Habsburg system [86].

Slovenian nationalists, meanwhile, worried about Slovenes' position relative to German-speakers. Recent historians of these and other Habsburg 'language frontiers' argue that the idea of these routinely bilingual areas as frontiers between different ethno-linguistic nations was actually novel to local residents – meaning nationalist activists had to alter residents' perceptions about language and identity to produce new conceptual boundaries of nationhood [80]. This argument challenges the very foundations of nationalist narratives about continuous ethnic communities, and what holds for one borderland region could equally be asked about Istria, Dalmatia or Vojvodina (the region north of Belgrade). Indeed, the so-called 'national indifference' approach [102], first applied to central Europe, has already started being applied to dynamics of national identification in the future Yugoslavia [57; 71]. The national identification problem recurred with Macedonia and Kosovo (Yugoslavia's future south-east), still within the Ottoman Empire in the late nineteenth century. Greece, Bulgaria and Serbia all aspired to expand into Macedonia by claiming its Orthodox population as members of *their* nations. All three states sent priests and teachers into Macedonia, and here too residents arguably came under pressure to declare for one nation or another.

In 1875–76, rebellions against Ottoman rule in Bosnia-Herzegovina and Bulgaria led to Russian intervention against the Ottoman Empire in 1877–78. The 1878 peace settlement made Bosnia-Herzegovina a protectorate of Austria–Hungary, putting a million more South Slavs under Habsburg administration. Habsburg authorities, viewing South Slav nationalisms as political challenges and security threats, tried to create a multi-faith Bosnian national identity as a counter-measure [74; 253]. Serbia gained the Toplica and Kosanica regions from the Ottoman Empire, but forced 71,000 Muslim inhabitants (49,000 Albanians) to leave; 60,000 Serbs moved from Ottoman areas to Serbia soon afterwards [97: 470]. Post-1878 Serbia, like its neighbours, continued aspiring to Ottoman territory claimed by its unification programme, while Albanian and Macedonian nationalist movements also formed. In 1912–13, Serbia, Bulgaria, Montenegro and Greece attacked the Ottoman Empire (the 'First Balkan War') shortly after Italy had invaded Ottoman lands in Libya. Serbia gained Kosovo and parts of Macedonia, and split the Sandžak region with Montenegro [89: 88]. Serb farmers received land in the conquered territories. The Serbian state viewed this as a war of liberation, whereas Albanians and Muslim Slavs felt conquered, even colonized [97: 474–8; 286: xlvi]. These opposed perceptions of Serbian rule fed into later debates about Kosovo's status within a Yugoslav state.

By the end of 1913, Bulgaria (trying to revise the Macedonian settlement) had fought a second war against Serbia, Greece, Romania, Montenegro and Turkey, while Albanian nationalists had declared independence from the Ottoman Empire. The peace treaties after the Balkan Wars confirmed a Kingdom of Albania [293: 84–5]. Any future expansion according to Serbia's national programme would involve winning South-Slav-inhabited lands from Austria–Hungary. Unification with Serbia did not yet interest mainstream South Slav politicians in Austria–Hungary, who pre-ferred (as reportedly did the Habsburg heir, Franz Ferdinand) to lobby for a South Slav unit complementing Austria and Hungary within the Empire. Much smaller radical movements, including 'Young Bosnia', did want unification with Serbia, and after the Habsburg annexation of Bosnia-Herzegovina in 1908, they received arms and encouragement from a group of Serbian military officers. Six Young Bosnia members, including Gavrilo Princip, assassinated Franz Ferdinand when he visited Sarajevo on 28 June 1914. The Habsburg government held Serbia responsible and implemented war plans, launching a cascade of declarations of war on both sides of the European alliance system [64].

Yugoslav unification

The main advocates for Yugoslav unification in 1914 were the 'Yugoslav Committee', a group of South Slav politicians who had fled Austria–Hungary, and the Serbian Prime Minister, Nikola Pašić, who declared in December 1914 that liberating the Slovenes, Croats and Serbs was Serbia's war aim. Pašić agreed co-operation with the Yugoslav Committee in July 1917 (the 'Corfu Declaration'). Pašić's intentions still matter today because they would help to answer a key problem in interpreting later Yugoslav history: whether Yugoslavia was designed to structurally favour the Serbs [58; 64; 65]. Yet the Pašić–Yugoslav Committee relationship – specifically, whether Pašić really wanted a Yugoslavia or just used 'Yugoslav' language to attain a Greater Serbia – has almost ended up overshadowing the South Slavs who remained in the Habsburg lands.

Prospects for Yugoslav unification fluctuated as the priorities of the Entente powers (Britain, France and Russia) changed, and as the wider war changed course [103]. Most troublingly, Entente promises made to Italy in April 1915 (the 'Treaty of London') directly contradicted South Slav national programmes, by awarding Italy most of the eastern Adriatic coast to satisfy Italy's own unification claim. Few Istrian South Slavs were Serbs, and the Yugoslav Committee feared Pašić might abandon them, especially after Bulgaria joined the Austro-German alliance and the Serbian army was forced to retreat to Corfu. Sensitivity about relations with Italy meant Britain and France supported the Yugoslav cause less than the Czechoslovak or Polish causes, even after having decided that Austria–Hungary should be broken up. By autumn 1918, Austria–Hungary had collapsed, and most of its national movements had declared independence. The South Slav movement was no exception.

On 29 October, South Slav National Councils in Ljubljana and Zagreb proclaimed an independent 'State of Slovenes, Croats and Serbs'. This unified on 1 December with the Kingdom of Serbia. The 'Podgorica Assembly' in Montenegro also voted (in November) to depose the Montenegrin king and join Serbia, in circumstances that remained controversial among supporters of a separate Montenegrin path [94: 321]. The 'Kingdom of Serbs, Croats and Slovenes' (colloquially 'Yugoslavia') now existed, ruled by Serbia's Karađorđević dynasty. The weighty question of how centralized or federalized it would be was deferred to a future Constituent Assembly. In the meantime, the Paris Peace Conference had to give international ratification to Yugoslavia's borders. The US president, Woodrow Wilson, who believed national self-determination in Europe would solidify peace, and Italy, which insisted that the Treaty of London should be honoured, although a Yugoslav state had appeared, clashed over Yugoslavia's case. Italy already controlled Istria and Zadar in December 1918, and in September 1919 a proto-Fascist Italian volunteer force even occupied Rijeka while the conference was deliberating. The fear of losing even more land helps explain why the National Councils unified with Serbia without awaiting constitutional guarantees.

Some authors argue the Great Powers themselves created Yugoslavia at Versailles because they wanted a buffer zone or economically dependent area in south-east Europe [19: 8–9; 65: 91–2; 101: 1181–85]. Yet since Habsburg authority in eastern Europe had internally disintegrated before the conference even convened, the 'created at Versailles' position seems overstated [64: 63–4]. The conference did, however, demonstrate that the international diplomatic principle for politically dividing space was based on majority national belonging. Disputes arose when people's national identities in an area were indeterminate or contested, and the Italo-Yugoslav border was just one such region.

Centralism prevailed over federalism in the 28 June 1921 Yugoslav constitution. The new state was a parliamentary democracy with universal male suffrage, and the 1920s have been called Yugoslavia's most democratic period until the 1990s – though only for men, since women could not vote [63: 74]. Moreover, the Yugoslav Communist Party (KPJ) was banned in 1921, and Macedonians and Albanians faced linguistic assimilation. Thousands of Muslim landowners, not only elites but also many Albanian peasants, lost their lands in Bosnia-Herzegovina, Macedonia and Kosovo [62: 80; 89: 96–8; 97: 480; 253: 145]. Yugoslavia's parliamentary life lasted until 1928, when a member of parliament shot the Croat Peasant Party leader Stjepan Radić and four others. King Aleksandar briefly tried to weather the ensuing constitutional crisis with a government led by the Slovenian politician Anton Korošec. In 1929 he introduced a royal dictatorship, banning all political parties and abolishing parliament. Aleksandar's 'unitarist' or 'integral' Yugoslavism aimed to supersede existing South Slav national identities and therefore repressed even harmless expressions of them, especially in non-Serb areas. It did not outlast his assassination in 1934 by émigré Macedonian and Croat ultra-nationalists.

Prince Paul, regent for Aleksandar's underage heir, decided Yugoslavia's constitutional problem had to be resolved after Hitler occupied Czechoslovakia in 1938. The 1935–39 Prime Minister, Milan Stojadinović, had drawn Yugoslavia closer to Italy and Germany. Paul removed Stojadinović in 1939 and sponsored the so-called 'compromise' between Stojadinović's replacement Dragiša Cvetković, a Serb, and Radić's successor Vladko Maček. Cvetković and Maček agreed to create an autonomous Croatian region (*banovina*), including large areas of historic Bosnia-Herzegovina. This turned away from centralism and integral Yugoslavism [63]. Whether the rest of Yugoslavia would have been similarly reordered cannot be known, since in March 1941 Hitler forced Yugoslavia into the Axis (the 'Tripartite Pact'). A group of Yugoslav army officers staged a coup against the pact, and Germany, Italy, Bulgaria and Hungary invaded Yugoslavia on 6 April. Assessing interwar Yugoslavia's instability has implications for later Yugoslav history: if the South Slav national programmes were already too incompatible in 1918 [58], post-1945 Yugoslavia would also have been doomed. If post-1918 events, not pre-1918 national antagonisms, destabilized interwar Yugoslavia [63], the idea of a South Slav state might not have been inherently flawed. Alternatively, it could also mean the Yugoslav idea did become permanently unworkable, but only later, as a result of interwar politics and the genocidal violence during 1941–45.

The Second World War in Yugoslavia

In April 1941, Germany, Italy, Hungary, Bulgaria and Albania (an Italian satellite) each annexed parts of Yugoslavia corresponding to their own expansionist national programmes. To administer what remained, they founded collaborationist puppet states with local leaders [61; 67; 82; 91; 100]. The part of Serbia under German military occupation had a 'Government of National Salvation', led by Milan Nedić from October 1941. The 'Independent State of Croatia' (NDH) was ostensibly sovereign. Its leader, Ante Pavelić, was the leader of the 'Ustaše', who had co-operated with the Macedonian nationalist group VMRO (Internal Macedonian Revolutionary Organization) in assassinating Aleksandar. The NDH adopted Pavelić's exclusivist ethnic ideology, which held that only Croats by blood had political rights, accepted Bosnian Muslims as Islamicized Croats, and believed that Serbs had to be converted to Catholicism, expelled or killed. It collaborated in the Holocaust and ran its own concentration camps (the largest at Jasenovac), in which hundreds of thousands of Jews, Serbs, Roma and political prisoners died. The Jasenovac death-toll was among the controversies reopened in 1980s Yugoslavia (Chapter 3).

1941–45 in Yugoslavia is sometimes described as a three-sided struggle for post-war control over territory [5: 52]. The NDH, envisaging a separate Croatia without minorities, was one side. Another was the forces commanded by Yugoslav military officers who stayed behind after the invasion. Commanded by Draža Mihailović and known as the 'Četniks' after nineteenth-century Serb groups that had fought Ottoman rule, they aimed to reinstate the Karađorđević dynasty in a homogenous, enlarged Yugoslavia centred on Serbia. The third side were the 'Partisans', the army of the KPJ, who began their uprising in July 1941. By November 1943 the KPJ, under Josip Broz Tito, was establishing Communist state structures in territory it controlled. The Anti-Fascist Council of the People's Liberation of Yugoslavia (AVNOJ) declared Communist Yugoslavia would be a republic, not a monarchy, and – correcting another major failing the KPJ perceived in pre-1941 Yugoslavia – federalized not centralized. All but one of this Yugoslavia's six republics would correspond to a South Slav people: Slovenia, Croatia, Montenegro, Macedonia, Bosnia-Herzegovina and Serbia (Vojvodina and Kosovo, with large Hungarian and Albanian populations, became autonomous within Serbia). Bosnia-Herzegovina, the exception, was conceived as a common republic of Serbs, Croats and Muslims [74: 297]. The Communists hoped to persuade non-Serbs that Yugoslavia could exist without Serb hegemony and to show workers and peasants that they would be emancipated.

Italy's capitulation in September 1943 greatly strengthened the Partisans, as did the Western Allies switching support from Mihailović to Tito and the Soviet push into the Balkans in 1944. The importance of interactions between internal forces, the Axis and the Allies is one reason why recent historians argue that the triangular civil-war approach misses important dynamics [71; 75]. Another reason is that other sides besides the main three – such as Bosnian Muslim autonomists, the Albanian anti-Communist organization Balli Kombëtar, and other groups in Slovenia and Montenegro – existed and pursued their own objectives during the occupation [91]. In addition, throughout Yugoslavia, there were more shifts of allegiance than a three-way ideological clash might suggest [75; 76].

Appreciating arguments about 1941–45 Yugoslavia is important for understanding the 1990s conflicts because 1941–45 was so often mentioned during the later wars. Nationalist historical narratives frequently retell national suffering and persecution by historic enemies, drawing the past and living memory into one unified narrative, and the Yugoslav region is no exception. Memories of mass violence in 1941–45 were widely recounted before and during the 1990s, when accusations about one people's genocidal intentions against another were expressed using partial narratives about past wars as evidence (Chapter 2). More distant history was similarly retold, creating endlessly repetitive narratives of the past [23; 112].

The Ustaše killed more than 300,000 Serbs – many in their own villages – and at least 75 per cent of Croatian and Bosnian Jews and Roma [67: 270–3; 74: 206–7]. Serbia's collaborationist governments co-operated in killing 29,000 Serbian Jews [61: 113–15].

The Četniks killed 65,000 Croats and Muslims in the NDH, mostly in Bosnia-Herzegovina, Dalmatia and Krajina [29: 146]. The Partisans expelled hundreds of thousands of Italians and Germans, and killed 5,000 Italians in mass graves [56: 281; 97: 482]. Partisan operations against Balli Kombëtar killed between 3,000 and 14,000 Albanians on the anti-Communist side [286: 312–13]. The largest Partisan crime occurred in May 1945, after the NDH's collapse. Tens of thousands of NDH personnel tried to surrender at Bleiburg (Austria) to British troops, who indicated they were the Partisans' responsibility. The Partisans forced them to march back to Yugoslavia [23: 170]. Debates about degrees of collaboration and resistance among the Četniks, Partisans and other forces have often escalated into arguments about the collective guilt of Croats, Bosniaks, Albanians or Serbs and the death-tolls for which each side or nation should be held responsible [23; 87].

Drawing on recent studies of the Holocaust and the Russian Revolution, several recent historians of Yugoslavia argue that scholars need microhistorical lenses on specific localities and patronage networks to understand how mass killing or revolutionary change was carried out [59; 71; 75; 82]. Connecting Yugoslavia with new approaches elsewhere in European history, these studies give the 1941–45 history of inter-ethnic relations a new complexity, emphasizing the short-term politics of collaborationism and occupation as the context for inter-ethnic violence as well as inter-ethnic solidarity [59; 66: 94; 74: 206–26]. Their findings suggest that microhistorical studies could also help understand the 1990s. Meanwhile, they reiterate the challenges the KPJ faced in establishing a second Yugoslav state.

Tito's Yugoslavia

The second Yugoslavia's society and state structure would not be stable unless the KPJ could resolve conflicts from the previous periods, especially 1941–45, and create unifying identities among Yugoslavia's people [10]. It began by establishing a one-party state using a similar Stalinist pattern to other Communist Parties in eastern Europe (indeed earlier than most), using trials of 'fascists' to eliminate not only Mihailović but also the democratic opposition from politics. It expropriated the lands of Germans, large landowners and the Church and distributed these to peasant Partisan veterans [1: 126–7]. Its demanding central economic plan required obligatory agricultural contributions from peasants, but this often failed. Small anti-Communist insurrections continued into the 1950s, especially in Kosovo [22: 242–5; 286: 312]. Yet the Party had support: among peasants from Herzegovina and Krajina who were resettled on the more fertile land in Slavonia and Vojvodina formerly owned by Germans; among women, who received the vote; among those who saw this Yugoslavia's multi-ethnic, federal structure as a guarantee against repression by Serbs or Croats [75; 100].

The idea that the Partisans liberated Yugoslavia from fascism without Soviet assistance underpinned their legitimating narrative of the 'people's liberation struggle', supposedly a victory by heroic anti-fascists over foreign fascists and 'domestic traitors' [28: 97]. The same idea gave Tito confidence in foreign policy. In May 1945 the Partisans had claimed Trieste, another port in the Italo-South Slav borderland, for Yugoslavia, causing a diplomatic crisis with the Allies until 1954. The Trieste crisis spotlighted problems of how states determine ethno-national identities and how refugees remember atrocities, so warrants consideration from historians concerned with the 1990s, even though the eastern Adriatic was not a live political issue later [56]. After Trieste, Tito made further assertive foreign policy moves, drawing Bulgaria and Albania closer as allies and planning intervention in the Greek Civil War. Yugoslav Communists, believing themselves successful Stalinists, were shocked when Stalin expelled Yugoslavia from the Soviet bloc in June 1948.

Initially, the KPJ tightened its Stalinism, imprisoning at least 16,000 suspected Stalin loyalists in harsh prison camps (the largest was an island, 'Goli Otok') and trying to intensify agricultural collectivization [22: 252]. An agrarian uprising in Cazinska Krajina (north-west Bosnia) in May 1950 demonstrated that peasants would resist this. In 1950–53, however, the KPJ revealed an ideological shift. The Party theorist Edvard Kardelj conceived the 'workers' self-management' system, with 'workers' councils' running Party-owned firms and organizations. Introduced in 1950, it became as symbolic of Tito's system as the Partisan narrative was [79: 60; 123: 151–7; 423: 133]. The KPJ abolished the failed collectivization policy [1: 129–31]. It also renamed itself the 'League of

Communists of Yugoslavia' (SKJ), symbolically rejecting Stalinist centralism (Kardelj was revisiting Marx's anticipated 'withering away of the state') [79; 115: 36]. Colloquially, it was still 'the Party'. All Party voluntary organizations merged into the 'Socialist Alliance of the Working People of Yugoslavia', including its wartime women's organization, the Anti-Fascist Front of Women. The ambiguous principle of 'brotherhood and unity' represented a concept of Yugoslav identity based on a multi-national 'working class of Yugoslavia', whereas expressions of single-nation patriotism attracted the attention of the security services. Meanwhile, the imprisonment of Tito's former comrade-in-arms, Milovan Đilas, for criticizing inner-circle Party elitism, was an important brake on internal dissent [32: 175]. In foreign policy, Yugoslavia joined India, Egypt, Indonesia, Ghana and Burma in founding the 'Non-Aligned Movement', which declared itself outside both superpower blocs. Tito's diplomatic prestige contributed to his personality cult within Yugoslavia.

In the early 1960s, the SKJ made liberal reforms permitting small privately-owned enterprises and easier travel across Yugoslav borders. Yugoslavs began enjoying higher living standards and greater availability of consumer goods than their Soviet-bloc counterparts. Though Communists worried about how much westernization this might bring, Yugoslavia's 'socialist consumerism' strengthened the regime: it had legitimacy at least while it could guarantee this standard of living [90]. Liberalism, however, did not go unopposed: a centralist SKJ faction around Aleksandar Ranković, the Interior Minister who controlled the security services, resisted it until 1966 when Tito purged Ranković from power. Ranković's fall permitted further experiments with liberalization, decentralization and even, briefly, more single-nation nationalism than the Party allowed before or since.

1968–69 saw multiple expressions of dissent inside and outside the Party [77; 95]. Belgrade students occupied their university in June 1968, demanding the SKJ act to reduce socio-economic inequalities. Albanians in Kosovo called for Kosovo to become a republic, not an autonomous province of Serbia. Slovenian Communists openly challenged the federation's decision to invest less in Slovenian road-building than elsewhere. Some Montenegrin intellectuals argued Montenegrin should be recognized as its own language. Party leaders in Croatia, meanwhile, were permitting unprecedented levels of mass participation in questioning the power-balance between Yugoslav peoples and republics, such as whether the Croatian language really had equal status in Yugoslavia and whether Croatia was getting to keep its fair share of foreign currency from tourism. The Croatian Catholic Church was now able to organize larger public gatherings than it ever previously could under Communism [28: 57–65]. The 'Croatian Spring' lasted until December 1971, when Tito dismissed the leaders who had permitted it (Savka Dabčević-Kučar, Mika Tripalo and Pero Pirker) [77].

Tito's rollback of the Croatian Spring and of liberalism in Serbia (where he dismissed the Party leaders Latinka Perović and Marko Nikezić in 1972) ended the dissent experiment [11]. Decentralization experiments, however, continued [96]. Constitutional amendments in 1968 gave republics more autonomy. The SKJ promoted Montenegrin, Macedonian and 'Muslim' national identities and histories as counterweights to the Serb–Croat relationship, and supported a separate Macedonian Orthodox Church [28: 12–13; 92: 130–3; 211]. The most radical decentralizing moves were Kardelj's 1974 constitution (a complex system of indirect participatory democracy) and a 1976 law breaking large companies into multiple workers' councils. Dejan Jović, criticizing the 1974 arrangements, argues that the only thing unifying post-1974 Yugoslavia was an elite ideological consensus: when that collapsed after Tito died on 4 May 1980, it left Yugoslavia vulnerable to disintegration [79]. Another critic accused the constitution of 'opening [...] the Pandora's box of nationalism' by putting each republic's undemocratic Party elites in charge of solving that republic's socio-economic problems [32: 8]. Conversely, a supportive view of the 1974 constitution considers it expressed 'the wishes of the majority of its peoples' and could have functioned if politicians and the army had defended it [26: 9–10]. The 1974 constitution poses historians of the 1990s two problems. One is whether it made Yugoslavia so structurally weak that its disintegration became inevitable. The other, raising the stakes, is whether it took sovereignty away from Yugoslavia's republics and thus made Slovenian, Croatian and Bosnian secession in 1992 illegitimate. This controversy even reached the International Criminal Tribunal for the Former Yugoslavia (ICTY) during its first trial [388: 73].

Explaining Yugoslavia's fragility is not enough to explain the 1990s wars. The actions of responsible individuals must still be accounted for, and structural explanations become vulnerable to critique if they appear to downplay individual accountability, especially where the JNA and Milošević are concerned [134: 456–8]. The background to the collapse is nonetheless important, not least because narratives about the 1990s wars so often refer to historical precedents. It is also important to appreciate the multiple frameworks through which people at the time viewed events. The question of inter-ethnic relations has dominated the literature on socialist Yugoslavia since the Yugoslav wars began, if not earlier: in 1989, the social and economic historian John Allcock was already asking, 'Why have we come to accept that nationalism is so central to the explanation of the Yugoslav crisis?' [105: 208]. The national question is not the only question either, for socialist Yugoslavia or earlier periods, and equally important contemporaneous themes of dissent have only recently resurfaced in the literature [7]. For socialist Yugoslavia, these included social inequalities between the employed and the unemployed, as well as public demands for the socialist regime to live up to its egalitarian ideology and do away with privileged Party elites [104: 259–62; 107; 123]. The 1980s crisis revealed many weaknesses in how these challenges had been met.

2 The Break-Up of the Yugoslav Federation

In the 1980s, the League of Communists of Yugoslavia (SKJ)'s socio-economic promises hollowed out, Yugoslavia's ideological foundations were challenged, and individual nations' nationalisms became ever more prominent. Tito's political generation had mostly predeceased him, and younger officials could not match his charismatic wartime record or his generation's interpersonal ties [148: 45]. The reformists dismissed in 1972 might have been a 'lost generation' who could have met the crisis head-on, but they were not yet politically welcome back [11: 56]. Instead, the 1974 constitution had replaced Tito with a collective federal presidency (one representative from each republic and province) rather than promote any individual to Tito's status and seem to place a single republic and nation at the forefront. This collective presidency, though symbolizing 'brotherhood and unity', proved unequal to the economic and ideological crises of the 1980s [10]. Perhaps pre-1980 Yugoslavia was already doomed to fail; perhaps the crises were mishandled so badly that Yugoslavia disintegrated; perhaps it was destroyed deliberately, in the 'joint criminal enterprise' with which the International Criminal Tribunal for the Former Yugoslavia (ICTY) would later charge Slobodan Milošević. Historians' interpretations of the 1980s crisis reveal much about what they believe caused the 1990s wars.

The 1990s wars would not have happened if Yugoslavia had reformed its way out of the crisis of Communism, or if it had disintegrated in the same peaceful ways as Czechoslovakia and parts of the USSR. The bitterest arguments about 1980s Yugoslavia, inside and outside scholarship, are around blame. Did Milošević consciously scheme to destroy the federation and create a homogenous Serbian state by persecuting non-Serbs? Was Milošević a nationalist, or an opportunist who took advantage of nationalism? Were the Serb generals in the Yugoslav People's Army (JNA) just as culpable as Milošević? Some other narratives turned the tables entirely: should the Slovenian and Croatian sides be blamed for excessive self-interest, even outright chauvinism, in their leaders' demands for further autonomy? Relationships between leaders and the public also matter. Were people manipulated by the republics' leaders into supporting nationalist solutions? Were they simply disregarded? Or did certain leaders act with their electorates' consent and complicity, creating society-wide responsibility for the conflicts? This chapter on short-term dimensions to these questions starts in 1980. However, the symbolic rupture of Tito's death did not mean the Yugoslav crisis began then; its underlying economic causes had already developed.

The economic crisis

The 1973 international oil crisis seriously affected Yugoslavia [1: 93–6]. Higher oil prices increased the cost of energy needed for industrialization, and repaying the foreign debt Yugoslavia incurred for infrastructural investment now cost more. Meanwhile, Western European governments terminated guest-worker programmes, reducing foreign currency remittances into Yugoslavia and removing an alternative for unemployed Yugoslavs. Yugoslavia had to borrow more, at higher rates. It has been called '[d]e facto bankrupt' by 1979, and could not even afford to import industrial materials by 1982 [115; 119: 223]. Yugoslavia refinanced its debts with US$ 6bn of International Monetary Fund (IMF) loans, under conditions to be implemented by the new Prime Minister, Milka Planinc [26: 13–17; 38: 47]. Yugoslavia had to freeze investment in infrastructure and social services, maximize exports while restricting imports, and prevent loss-making enterprises keeping workers employed if they could fire them. Planinc's successor, Branko Mikulić, initially tried to halt the reforms but had to return to the IMF in 1988 [26: 101–5]. Unemployment and inflation rose and consumers' purchasing power declined, exposing Yugoslavs to a precarity that socialist 'progress' ought – or so Communism promised – to have been able to prevent.

25

Yugoslavia's socio-economic system, however, had its own vulnerabilities. Workers' councils, according to one eminent economist, had created an 'obsession' with voting that encouraged cliquishness yet prevented genuine discussion [118: 47–8]. Moreover, councils tended to invest profits in wage increases and job creation rather than growth (a problem to the extent that one considers constant economic growth to be a good thing). Two mid-1980s expert commissions investigated the economic crisis but could not bring themselves to challenge the fundamentals of self-management [32: 151–2; 148: 46; 262: 13–14]. The Party's response created a 'huge credibility gap' between officials and the public [115: 171]. John Lampe argues the most successful enterprises were those which did reinvest and stopped workers' councils mushrooming, but such a course could be politically difficult [22: 321]. He also challenges the argument about the IMF undermining the Yugoslav economy [19; 38], instead blaming Yugoslav politicians for not addressing regional disparities [83: 194]. The possibility that self-management was inadequate for Yugoslavia's economic sustainability has serious implications. Since self-management was Yugoslav socialism's ideological cornerstone, could Yugoslavia be re-imagined without it? Until recently [107; 141], the 1980s self-management controversies received much less scholarly attention than the concurrent undermining of official historical narratives. But both difficulties reflected a deeper weakness: the bases of Party legitimacy had collapsed.

This was an important precondition for the break-up, although explanations differ. Several 1980s Yugoslav sociologists blamed Yugoslavia's oligarchic political system for 'continually generating and deepening' the socio-economic crisis [32: 153]. Susan Woodward suggested 1980s socio-economic conditions destroyed a 'moderate political centre' that Yugoslav society's middle strata might have formed; instead, she argued, people turned to networks of family, friendship and patronage, becoming increasingly suspicious of perceived biases (including ethnic biases) against them [38: 54]. Patrick Patterson also referred to 1980s economic insecurity, but from a different angle. The 1960s–70s Party had directly encouraged (and borrowed heavily to finance) consumer aspirations that many 1980s consumers who had once enjoyed them could no longer achieve [90: 314–19]. The shock of precarity showed that Yugoslav socialism had failed to deliver on its promises [1: 206–8]. Yet the crisis did not affect all regions equally. Instead, it magnified those inequalities that the regime had not resolved, as became clear in 1981 when mass protests occurred in Kosovo.

The 1981 protests in Kosovo

Yugoslavia's overall economic indicators masked wide disparities. In 1981, Yugoslavia's average per-capita income was 89,466 dinars, but Slovenia's was 160,905 dinars. Croatia's and Vojvodina's were just under 115,000 dinars per capita, and Serbia was in the middle. Macedonia, Montenegro and Bosnia-Herzegovina averaged around 57,000–69,000, but Kosovo's average per capita income of 29,684 dinars fell below even that [287: 24]. Unemployment also worsened on a north–south axis. Slovenia had almost full employment in 1981 (1.6 per cent unemployment), and Kosovo again fared worst, with 39 per cent unemployment [123: 384]. Since 1965 a federal fund ('FADURK') had tried to redistribute money from richer republics/provinces to poorer ones, but it had not reversed inequality enough [1: 83–5; 22: 291]. The 1981 protests thus combined two long-running unsolved problems: Yugoslavia's regional disparities and Kosovo's status as a region, indeed Albanians' very status within Yugoslavia.

In 1968, Albanian students in Kosovo had protested for Kosovo to become a stand-alone republic. The Party rejected this but allowed their other demand, a full Albanian-language university in Priština [26: 27–9; 92: 83–4]. Intellectually, this stimulated 'a veritable Albanian national renaissance' [280: 38]. Economically, however, there were fewer jobs than new graduates expected [287: 25–9]. On 11 March 1981, 2,000 students in Priština began demonstrating against conditions in residences, soon adding the 'Kosovo republic' demand. When tens of thousands of Albanians in six cities joined the demonstrations on 1–2 April, the federal authorities declared a state of emergency and suppressed the protests under martial law. Another protest in mid-May curtailed the school year. The authorities' punitive and deterrent measures had longer-lasting consequences. Two hundred and twenty six demonstrators, mainly students and teachers, received multi-year sentences in semi-secret trials even for acts like painting slogans. Other protestors were fired, 600 people were expelled from the Party in Kosovo, and several leading Kosovar officials were replaced [24: 7–13; 287: 41–4]. Albanian-language rock music also came under suspicion [402: 347]. Over the next few years, 1,289 Albanians were imprisoned for political crimes, creating a '1981 generation' in underground militant movements and adding political pressure to economic reasons why young Albanians emigrated [288: 49; 291: 959–61].

The authorities' reactions in 1981 revealed an official 'script' or narrative for understanding social and political unrest: Yugoslav socialism most feared 'counter-revolution' (organized subversion), which the military, the security services and politicians understood they existed to guard against. They could not comprehend Albanian nationalism outside the context of Yugoslavia's hostile relationship with Enver Hoxha's regime in Albania, and believed Hoxha was deliberately stimulating Albanian nationalism to undermine Yugoslavia internally. Neither could they appreciate that demanding a Kosovo republic did not necessarily mean outright separatism, even though it might [29: 301]. The trials therefore treated demonstrators as organized militants. Julie Mertus argued the authorities' misrecognition of 'counter-revolution' stopped them addressing Kosovo's underlying inequalities and made them underestimate the immediate economic and political crisis [287: 32]. It might also have caused longer-term damage. One reason Kosovo was poor was because its abundant raw minerals were mostly exported for manufacturing elsewhere in Yugoslavia, since strategic factories in Kosovo would have been vulnerable in case of war with Albania [292: 285].

Branka Magaš argued the 1981 protests exposed an even deeper structural problem for the Yugoslav state. Constitutionally, each Yugoslav republic was linked to the national sovereignty of one South Slav people, or three (Croats, Muslims and Serbs) in Bosnia-Herzegovina. Croats, Serbs, Slovenes, Muslims, Macedonians and Montenegrins were Yugoslavia's constituent nations or peoples (*narodi*). Albanians, and others like Hungarians or Italians who had 'their own' nation-state outside Yugoslavia, were not *narodi*, only 'nationalities' (*narodnosti*) [322: 264–6]. Making Kosovo a republic implied more than detaching it from Serbia: it would have given Albanians the same recognition as each South Slav national identity. Whereas Stevan Pavlowitch, for instance, considered a 'Kosovo republic' infeasible because it would have triggered similar demands elsewhere in Yugoslavia [93: 186], Magaš argued 1980s Yugoslavia should have accepted a Kosovo republic as part of its reforms. In 1982, she called it 'untenable to treat a population which will within two years be the third largest nationality as a "national minority"' [24: 38]. This would have overturned the idea of Yugoslavia being the state of the six constituent South Slav peoples and raised questions about how to accommodate the Albanians of western Macedonia. It was practically unthinkable to most politicians outside Kosovo [282: 9–10].

The crisis of historical interpretation

A second public scandal about Kosovo involved the estimated 30,000 Serbs and Montenegrins who left Kosovo in 1981–87 [26: 32–4; 120; 287: 41–2]. The Albanian perspective was that Serbs left for regions with higher incomes and more jobs. However, some emigrants gave interviews in Serbia which accused the Party of not protecting minorities from discrimination if a rival ethnic group dominated a Party branch. In 1985, a group of Serb activists in Kosovo Polje started publicizing this claim [148: 89–94]. Emigrant narratives accused the Kosovo Party of intentionally favouring Albanians over Serbs since 1968, Albanians of disloyalty to Yugoslavia, and Albanian families of deliberately having more children to outnumber – and eventually be able to expel – Serbs [114: 118–20]. Around Serbia, these explanations circulated in academic sociology [32: 189–97], in literature, and in the mass media, which used allegations of Albanians' sexual violence against Serbs to imply a need to restore 'national dignity and masculine honour' [110: 569]. The emigration and persecution narratives had become incompatible with explanations about economic decline. The emigrants' interviews had entered a public sphere where official interpretations of the past were being drastically reinterpreted, increasingly sensationalistically, leading to what Jasna Dragović-Soso calls a 'breakdown of official historiography' [114: 65].

Communist Yugoslavia's simplistic official narrative about 1941–45 obscured many Yugoslavs' shifting allegiances during that time and masked Partisan retaliation altogether. Openly anti-Communist publications circulated among émigrés in the diaspora, but possessing them in Yugoslavia could mean prison. A republic's authorities might sometimes relax ideological boundaries, notably during the Croatian Spring, but Party leaderships and cultural institutions took their ideological-watchdog role seriously. In 1968, the Serbian author Dobrica Ćosić, a critic of decentralization and economic liberalization, was expelled from the Party for criticizing Kosovo's and Vojvodina's growing autonomy; his opponents thought this dangerously close to Serbian nationalism [126: 187]. Ćosić re-entered public historical commentary in 1977 with a novel about 1914–18 which controversially suggested Serbs had erred by joining Yugoslavia not a dedicated Serbian state. It anticipated the tone of many mid-1980s works. Indeed, by 1983 publishing had already changed enough that Ćosić could include his formerly-suppressed speeches in a new collection [114: 92–3].

The breakdown of official history was catalyzed by a 1981 biography of Tito by one of his own Partisan comrades, Vladimir Dedijer, with details that chipped Tito's legendary infallibility away. Whether the demystification was accidental [114: 78–80] or intentional [40: 48–9; 92: 135], it gave publishers confidence to support creative and academic works that challenged the official narratives in increasingly sensational, even antagonistic, ways. The media joined in, beginning with the Belgrade weekly *NIN*'s 1982 articles about Goli Otok. Other works explored the persecution of 'Cominformists', the validity of socialist Yugoslavia's internal borders, whether national sacrifices in 1914–18 had been worthwhile, and – the late 1980s' most prominent theme – the mass killings of 1941–45 [23]. Among religious believers, mass events organized by the Croatian and Serbian Churches amplified these narratives [28].

The 1980s undermining of Yugoslav historiography is often put down to Tito's death weakening the Party so much that it could no longer impose its own narrative on the public. In one sense, however, Yugoslav Communism might have done too *little* to communicate its narrative: education, including history and literature (new Yugoslavs' core historical and cultural knowledge), had been devolved to republics since 1948, with no central control over what different republics' students learned about Yugoslavia's origins. In 1981, the Yugoslav Writers' Union proposed a new common core for literature containing a nationally-diverse selection of authors, to become half of any republic or province's literature curriculum. Other writers objected to its balance of languages, its projection of present-day ethno-territorial belonging on to historical figures, and – the chief objection of the Slovenian Writers' Union in 1983 – whether the state should prescribe a central curriculum anyway. The proposal was shelved in 1986, another symbolic indicator of the inability to agree a Yugoslav identity based on a shared past [122]. Looking only at schools, however, leaves out institutions that Communists viewed as equally responsible for education, such as the Party youth organization and, for young men, the army [167]. More research is still needed on how these institutions too presented Yugoslavia's past and present.

The mid-1980s history/politics nexus

The simplification of history to legitimize Party rule meant that events which did not fit that framework lived on as semi-private local knowledge and rumour [116; 344]. 'Victims of Fascism' were widely commemorated, but specifically ethno-political dimensions of violence in 1941–45 were not. Artistic and academic revisiting of the past, however, suddenly made ethno-political mass violence a public topic in the mid-1980s. Bette Denich's study of what she called the 'symbolic revival of genocide' used the example of a 1982 play by Jovan Radulović that dramatized an Ustaša massacre of Serbs in Krajina [112: 367]. The Vojvodina Party banned it for so-called 'Greater Serbian chauvinism'. Amid intellectual debate over implications for freedom of expression, the Serbian and Slovenian Party branches both allowed its performance in 1983 [114: 105–6].

By the mid-1980s, official Yugoslav figures for the 1941–45 war dead were also being questioned. The official figure was 1.7 million, but this included estimated demographic effects (from disease, and children not being born) as well as actual deaths. The inflated statistic had appeared to qualify Yugoslavia for greater reparations and magnified the Partisans' sacrifices. The overstatement needed correcting; the problem was what figures were correct [23: 161]. Two demographers working independently, Bogoljub Kočović in 1985 and Vladimir Žerjavić in 1989, each calculated that just over one million people from Yugoslavia had been killed (Kočović quoted 1,014,000, Žerjavić 1,027,000). Scholars with different interpretations of Yugoslav history still concur on the one million figure [5: 45; 22: 440; 29: 161; 67: 270–3; 74: 255–6; 113: 132; 216: 9; 221: 185–6]. At the same time, however, many more divergent estimates were being published. They tended to maximize deaths suffered by the writer's own nation and minimize the number of people that the writer's nation could be said to have killed, in order to influence perceptions of the greatest victims and worst aggressors. In this respect, the broad agreement between Kočović (a Serb) and Žerjavić (a Croat) helped give their figures weight.

The most debated document in the history/politics nexus is the Serbian Academy of Sciences and Arts (SANU) memorandum on the Yugoslav crisis, a leaked draft of which appeared in September 1986. Its first section blamed 1960s economic liberalization, the 1974 constitution and Kardelj's reforms for the crisis. The second, on Serbia and the Serbs, accused Slovenia and Croatia of 'political and economic domination' over Serbia and spoke of a 'physical, political, legal, and cultural genocide' by Albanian nationalists against Serbs in Kosovo. It then extended the Kosovo Serb question Yugoslavia-wide by warning that Serbs in Croatia had never been 'as endangered in the past as they are today' except under the Independent State of Croatia (NDH) [111: 56]. The SANU Memorandum is a key item of evidence in arguments that Yugoslavia was deliberately destroyed according to a Serb nationalist programme. Some scholars see it as that programme's intellectual or ideological foundation [26: 40; 29: 320–1; 33: 46; 165: 40; 216: 23]. A few even present it alongside Garašanin's foreign policy and 1941 Četnik directives as evidence of a continuous history of Serbian expansionism against Muslim Slavs and Albanians [129; 206: 21–3]. Audrey Helfant Budding's study of the Memorandum, however, interpreted it as attempting to solve Yugoslavia's crisis rather than dissolve Yugoslavia – though its authors' commitment to recentralization would lead them to support Milošević rather than defend Yugoslavia in its entirety [111: 57–60].

The Memorandum's ideas were not novel; it gave collective intellectual authority to existing arguments. Even its most shocking claim, about Albanian/Croat genocidal intentions against Serbs, had already been voiced, by 21 Serbian priests who accused

Albanians of genocide in Kosovo in May 1982. A few months before the Memorandum, the historian Vasilije Krestić – who supposedly wrote the Memorandum's historical sections – published an article charging Albanians and Croats with genocide against Serbs [28: 123–5; 114: 185]. Dragović-Soso thus argued the Memorandum was part of a broader context of crisis and revisionism, in which the weeks of denunciations it received strengthened its agenda-setting power [114: 188].

Political elites and the public

The SANU Memorandum is an obvious focal point for the 1980s crisis if questions about ethnicity and nationalism are the most important – and these do need to be visible, since so many wartime aims were expressed in ethno-nationalist terms. However, there has been less scrutiny of contemporaneous events that revealed equally troubling flaws in the Yugoslav system but were not so easily connectable to ethno-nationalist agendas. A major example is the 1987 'Agrokomerc' scandal which ended up discrediting Bosnia-Herzegovina's Communist leaders. By then, Agrokomerc contributed 75 per cent of Bosnia-Herzegovina's agricultural exports and dominated the economy of its home region, Cazinska Krajina [203: 58]. Investigators discovered Agrokomerc had funded itself with promissory notes based on non-existent money. The Bosnian Party leader, Hamdija Pozderac, and his allies had taken great credit for Agrokomerc's success and now had to resign. The Agrokomerc scandal does usually appear in accounts of 1980s Bosnian politics [26: 41–2; 29: 336; 38: 87; 221: 48; 223: 196–8; 241: 209–11; 262: 101]. However, Neven Andjelić argued its full impact was generally underestimated. The scandal did not just remove experienced Party leaders but also an entire slice of the republic's financial, industrial and media elite. The unprecedented initiative permitted to the Bosnian press in reporting the scandal opened up more space for public political discussion than had previously been possible under Communism there [203: 79–99]. This therefore created the space in which Croat, Muslim/Bosniak and Serb nationalist parties could start encouraging the Bosnian public to vote according to ethno-national group interests in 1989–91.

Intellectual and cultural discussion had also opened up in Slovenia, where Slovenian Communists were consciously allowing it. Youth subcultures and alternative social movements (including punk bands, feminist associations and Yugoslavia's first gay organization, Magnus) found a supportive conduit to the Party through the League of Socialist Youth of Slovenia [413: 485]. This organization had refused advice to repress punk in 1980–81. Its magazine *Mladina* (*Youth*) became politically influential as Slovenia's alternative scene widened into a larger pro-democratization movement [175: 374–5]. The Slovenian Party endorsed these developments in 1986 by selecting Milan Kučan, part of a younger generation of Communists, as its new leader. Kučan was prepared to support and eventually even amplify Slovenian civil society's arguments. In this environment, the Slovenian intellectual journal *Nova revija* (*New Review*) could publish 'Contributions for a Slovenian National Programme' in January 1987. This document could be read alongside the SANU Memorandum as position-statements from Yugoslavia's 'two most active intellectual oppositions', in Serbia and Slovenia [114: 177]. It argued that Slovenes would be economically better off without Slovenia having to subsidize less-developed republics and provinces, that the Slovene language had second-class status, and that Slovenia's low birth-rate was worrying. Two months later, the Association of Slovenian Writers proposed amendments to the Yugoslav constitution which would make republics more independent from the centre and end the SKJ's political monopoly. An ambitious political programme of further decentralization as well as multi-party democracy was therefore emerging from Slovenia.

The clash between the Yugoslav federal authorities and Slovenia's reformists and nationalists came in May 1988, when the state security service arrested three *Mladina* journalists and a whistleblowing conscript for leaking an internal JNA plan about how to declare a state of emergency in Slovenia. Slovenian social movements and newspapers had already been criticizing the JNA and the defence minister, Branko Mamula, for selling arms to Ethiopia during the famine there and using conscript labour for building his holiday home. The JNA saw its mission as defending a centralized Yugoslavia, and suspicious military leaders saw Slovenia as a source of subversion [152]. The Slovenian media and public rallied behind the *Mladina* four – not least because their military trial was conducted in Serbo-Croatian not Slovenian [194: 153–4]. With public demonstrations outside the courthouse for weeks, and a new Committee for the Defence of Human Rights ready to become an opposition umbrella organization in 1989, the *Mladina* trial was a turning point for public political mobilization in Slovenia [26: 67–9]. A more critical view, however, argues it 'allowed all questions on the [Slovenian] public agenda before 1989 to be subsumed into the national question', marginalizing other social and environmental problems the alternative movements had identified [197: 148]. Slovenia provides one opportunity for considering how nationalism became a particular republic's dominant framework for explaining the crisis. The most studied republic in this respect, however, is Serbia, where understanding the elite/public relationship is essential for accounting for Milošević's rise to power.

Milošević had been a director in the energy and banking sectors before entering politics full-time in 1984 as the head of the SKJ in Belgrade [33: 24–33]. He moved up to chair the Serbian branch of the SKJ in 1986. In April 1987, he made an official visit to a closed Party meeting in Kosovo Polje, where the 1985 petition campaign had begun. His words 'Nobody is allowed to beat you' were filmed when he spoke to some of the 15,000 Serb demonstrators outside. He listened to them overnight and argued at the next Serbian Party meeting that the Party should act on their demands [131]. He then organized support within the Serbian media and, at the next Serbian Party plenum in September 1987, ousted his former political patron Ivan Stambolić as president of Serbia [33: 47–9; 262: 22] – an outcome which Christopher Bennett viewed as 'the decisive battle in Yugoslavia's disintegration' even though it came four years before the JNA operations against Slovenia and Croatia [5: 94]. Milošević's actions from 1987 onwards were based, more than any Yugoslav Communist contemporaries except eventually Kučan, on a strategy of *mass* politics and communication. His post-1987 speeches amplified existing public arguments about Serbs' status, emphasized a narrative of Serbs' historical victimhood, and incorporated characteristic Serbian folk language. All this differed greatly from most Communist politicians' technical jargon [35; 128; 130; 142; 148]. A key text in interpreting Milošević's communication is his Kosovo battlefield anniversary speech in June 1989, which took the mythic narrative about disunity losing Serbia the battle and accused Serbian Communist elites of similar present-day disunity. Nebojša Vladisavljević read this as a change of strategy [148: 178], and Florian Bieber as 'the symbolic culmination of [Milošević's] process of mass mobilization' [124: 100].

Milošević said he was offering the Serbian public an 'anti-bureaucratic revolution'. He was also carrying it out through them. His public 'rallies of solidarity' in 1988–89 were not just communicative events but also direct political pressure on rivals, even though he seems to have co-opted the protest rally format rather than initiating it altogether [148: 166–70]. In September 1988, the Serbian Party rejected federal guidelines about quietening public mobilization [148: 146–7]. In October, 100,000 people in Novi Sad and 25,000 in Titograd (now Podgorica) joined demonstrations outside the provincial assemblies. These forced out Vojvodina's Party leaders immediately, while the Montenegrin leaders took three further months and more demonstrations to remove [148: 157–66; 262: 31–3]. Milošević allies replaced both leaderships. It was the same in Kosovo, although miners at Trepča unsuccessfully went on hunger-strike against Milošević altering Kosovo's constitutional status. In March 1989, amendments to the Serbian constitution revoked the autonomy of Vojvodina and Kosovo, fulfilling a major objective for the recentralization lobby. By exerting pressure outside his own republic and making radical constitutional changes, Milošević escalated the Yugoslav constitutional crisis and gave supporters of decentralization ever more grounds for fearing a state more strongly centred on Belgrade.

Milošević, Kučan and the end of the Party

No figure in the Yugoslav wars receives more scholarly attention than Milošević [134: 446]. Indeed, the very amount of coverage he should receive relative to other factors is contentious. Sabrina Ramet stated that '[f]or most analysts [...] there is no doubt concerning the incendiary role played by Milošević and his associates', and criticizes authors who do not emphasize it, including Susan Woodward and Robert Hayden [53: 5–6]. Woodward disagreed that Milošević's aggression made Yugoslavia break up,

arguing instead that Yugoslav federal authority had already broken down as Cold War economic and diplomatic systems collapsed
[38: 14–22]. Hayden, whose book on constitutional nationalism
did not discuss Milošević prominently, said that Milošević's 'one-
man rule' made Serbia's constitutions not 'very relevant' to his
work [17: 21]. Their disagreement became one of the longest running in the literature on the Yugoslav wars.

Other lenses beyond an individual spotlight on Milošević were
nevertheless helpful for understanding what was happening in
Serbia, let alone the rest of Yugoslavia. Recognizing them did not
prevent historians holding individuals accountable for aggressive
actions and language when this is needed; yet focusing solely on
individuals (a drawback, for instance, of popular accounts that
sensationalize Milošević and his marriage) would omit important
institutional and structural factors in the break-up [252: 12]. More
has been written on how Milošević manipulated the public than
on the public themselves or even on other institutions that coop-
erated with him. This is a striking gap in the literature unless one
should just assume that people were brainwashed and did what
they were told, though Vladisavljević's study of popular participation in the 'anti-bureaucratic revolution' helps fill it [148]. More
generally, historians could still stand to know much more about
how social and national demands intersected in late-1980s Serbia,
or indeed anywhere else in Yugoslavia [107; 160].

A good example of how studying the public could deepen
understandings of Milošević came from Goran Musić's research
on Belgrade factory workers. Musić found that workers in the
Rakovica district of Belgrade, through their union, had been proposing reforms to the Yugoslav system since 1984. They did wish
some recentralization of the federation, but these demands did
not intersect with ethno-nationalist grievances until autumn 1988.
Moreover, before the factory workers' demonstration outside
the Federal Assembly in October 1988 (famously addressed by
Milošević), others that same summer had been about class interests rather than the national question, such as asking for over-
paid managers to be sacked because they were not workers – but
Milošević had chosen to ignore these [141]. Rather than assum-
ing that post-Tito politics *would* become a rush towards nationalism, this argument foregrounded what alternative programmes
existed, how they were defeated and why.

By 1989, the two main federal-reform programmes already reflected the arguments of Serb and Slovenian nationalist movements: Milošević's recentralization against the Slovenian programme of greater republican autonomy. In 1989 the programmes directly confronted each other. During the Trepča miners' strike in February 1989, Slovenian intellectuals organized a support rally. Kučan addressed it, stating that the miners were defending 'AVNOJ' Yugoslavia, and TV Ljubljana broadcast it live [114: 224]. Kučan's speech breached the weakening convention of republican leaders not intervening in other republics' affairs, and implied that Milošević was the deviator from Tito's legitimate path [38: 98]. In July 1989, the Slovenian Party proposed amending Slovenia's constitution to assert the sovereignty of the Slovenian republic and nation, including the right to secession, and to permit Slovenia free elections. A Serbian newspaper published the amendments in August and they intensified the constitutional crisis. The Socialist Alliance in Serbia endorsed a boycott of Slovenian consumer goods, protesting against the amendments and against Slovenia banning a Milošević rally in Ljubljana [17: 35–8; 22: 353–4; 262: 57–8].

This dispute overshadowed the next federal SKJ Congress, in January 1990. So did events in 1989 which had ended monopolistic Communist rule in many eastern European countries: Hungary had introduced multi-party democracy, Poland had held semi-free elections, the Velvet Revolution had succeeded in Czechoslovakia and Nicolae Ceauşescu had been brought down in Romania. One Soviet republic, Lithuania, had also ended the Communist political monopoly within its borders. Most dramatically, the Berlin Wall had fallen in November 1989. The January 1990 congress should have reformed the SKJ so that it too could function in a multi-party system. However, every Slovenian proposal was rejected [A34: 80]. The Slovenian delegation left, believing Milošević had always intended to reject the plans. The Croatian delegates followed them, led by the Croatian Party's new leader, Ivica Račan. The Congress did not just mark the federal Party's breakdown but openly aligned Croatia's leadership with the Slovenian position [262: 72]. Secession by Croatia, as well as Slovenia, was now possible.

Who should be blamed for making Yugoslavia ungovernable by 1990? The case against Milošević is strong [29; 33; 34; 134; 262].

Within this, some historians argue that his aim in 1990 was to govern the whole of Yugoslavia repressively and others argue that he already intended to provoke war so that Serbia could expand into the Croatian and Bosnian republics (Chapter 3). The counterargument blames Slovenia and Kučan. These opposing views appear in interpretations of the 1989 Slovenian constitutional amendments. One interpretation sees them as a proto-democratic reaction to Milošević's authoritarian behaviour and the risk of JNA intervention against Slovenia [26: 119; 193: 238]. Hayden, conversely, views them as a Slovenian choice to 'withdraw from Yugoslavia' and seal the federation's fate [17: 30]. Interpreting the balance of responsibility depends on how the reader ethically assesses the options open to Slovenia's leaders in 1989. Were they obliged to act with pan-Yugoslav interests in mind, and especially to consider the impact Slovenian separatism might have on Croatia and its Serb minority? Or, in the context of events in the federation since 1987, was their foremost responsibility to protect Slovenian interests? And had Milošević already constrained Slovenian actions by undermining Montenegro, Vojvodina and Kosovo? Slovenia and Croatia both declared independence in June 1991, 18 months after the disastrous Congress. Those 18 months have received detailed scrutiny to explain why the final disintegration of Yugoslavia occurred through war.

3 From Crisis to War in Slovenia and Croatia

The federal Party's collapse forced existing leaders, and their rivals, to adjust to multi-party elections in each republic. These would bring nationalist parties into government in Slovenia, Croatia, Bosnia-Herzegovina and Macedonia, and rubber-stamp Milošević's political control in Serbia and Montenegro. Meanwhile, the federation's Prime Minister, Ante Marković, was trying to reconstruct Yugoslav politics around an alternative pro-gramme to Milošević's assault on the republics' sovereignty. To explain why the break-up of Yugoslavia led to war, historians must interpret the political conflicts and failed alternatives of 1990: these would set the course for the decisions about independence and use of force that leaders in Slovenia, Croatia and Belgrade took in 1991.

From Slovenian viewpoints, Milošević's programme threatened Slovenia's economic prosperity as well as the status of Slovenian language and culture. For Croatia, stakes were even higher. Croatia, unlike Slovenia, had a substantial Serb population, especially near the borders with Bosnia-Herzegovina and Serbia. Milošević's open constitutional revision suggested these areas could be his next target, especially if Croatia appeared likely to secede. Against this background, the openly nationalist Croatian Democratic Union (HDZ) won Croatia's April–May 1990 elections. Croatian Serbs who sympathized with Milošević first used violence on 17 August 1990, when they kept Croatian police out of Knin with roadblocks, after which the Croatian authorities resolved to militarize the police as a future national defence force. The Knin roadblocks, sometimes called the 'log revolution', are among the events that could mark the start of the Yugoslav wars, Ivo Goldstein for instance noting them as 'the beginning of the aggression against Croatia' [70: 218]. By spring 1991, the Serb

Democratic Party (SDS) in Croatia was regularly attempting to take control of towns in Krajina and Eastern Slavonia, and the Yugoslav People's Army (JNA) was visibly taking that side.

The JNA's open mobilization in support of Milošević and SDS, against Slovenia and Croatia, occurred two days after Slovenia and Croatia declared independence in June 1991. After ten days in Slovenia, where the JNA could not prevent Slovenian forces taking over border-posts, JNA operations shifted to Croatia. Here, war lasted until August 1995, with the JNA and Serbian interior ministry propping up the authority known as the 'Republic of Serb Krajina' which had occupied one-third of Croatian territory. The Croatian war of independence, called the 'Homeland War' in Croatian, provides the post-Yugoslav Croatian state's founding myth, yet it was also a time of enforced public consensus around Croatian patriotism and a time when Serbs were persecuted in the name of the Croatian nation. Less forcefully, and without the pressure of ongoing war, the Slovenian state also took steps to strengthen its national identity. The break-up of Yugoslavia thus involved multiple, deliberate underminings of non-national alternatives for social and political identification, a process which accelerated throughout 1990 and 1991.

The Slovenian and Croatian multi-party elections

Yugoslavia's republics held multi-party elections at different times, with Slovenia first, in April 1990. The result split power between Lojze Peterle's non-Communist opposition coalition (DEMOS), which won the parliamentary elections, and Milan Kučan, who became president [194: 156]. Croatia, with more complex electoral politics, presented several possibilities for who would end up confronting Milošević. Ivica Račan was reorienting the Croatian Communists as the social-democratic 'Party of Democratic Change' (SDP), and his democratization relaxed the official suspicion of Croatian patriotic and religious expression that had typified Croatian politics since 1972. Another strong contender was a liberal coalition organized by Savka Dabčević-Kučar and Mika Tripalo, the very leaders Tito had dismissed then; journalists and musicians, unsurprisingly, started speaking of a second 'Croatian Spring'. The politician who gained most from Račan's democratization, however, was the former dissident historian Franjo Tuđman.

In June 1989, Tuđman, well-funded by Croats abroad, had founded HDZ, which aimed to unify Croats into a national movement. Its first congress was on 24–25 February 1990. Amid the Yugoslav constitutional crisis, Tuđman's assertive speeches about Croats' history of statehood set the intra-Croatian electoral agenda and positioned him as defending Croatian interests against Milošević. HDZ won the Croatian elections and elected Tuđman president on 30 May. Croatia's electoral law, however, magnified the winning party's advantage – a system designed by the Croatian Communists but accidentally benefiting the rival they had initially dismissed [24: 256; 262: 82]. HDZ's two-thirds parliamentary majority (54 of 80 seats) and consequent say over the presidency reflected only 42 per cent of votes, ahead of 35 per cent for SDP and 15 per cent for Dabčević-Kučar's coalition [22: 360]. The president who claimed to be uniting all Croats, and whose role in the wars is still disputed, had had a smaller share of votes than his rhetoric suggested.

Even among Croats, views were divided over Tuđman's anti-Communism and his controversial professional record. In 1987 he had given a very low figure, 30,000–40,000, for deaths at Jasenovac (as opposed to the 83,000 suggested by Kočović/Žerjavić). His writing contributed to the polemical competition between Serb deaths at Jasenovac and Croat deaths at Bleiburg sustained by authors and the Serbian and Croatian Churches in 1988–90 [23; 28; 87; 109; 116; 121]. Tuđman's defenders argue he was misrepresented by scholars who sympathized with Yugoslavia [180: 250], but amid the 1988–90 debates his wider argument – that, since genocide was a primordial constant in human history, there was no point holding specific ideologies or people accountable – was nonetheless alarming [369: 1204].

Scholars have also debated whether Tuđman's very presence in power contributed to Croatian Serb fears about living in a Croatian republic. Again Hayden and Ramet disagreed: Hayden argued Serbs were justified in fearing that Tuđman would silence the history of the mass killing of Serbs by the Independent State of Croatia (NDH), whereas Ramet attributed Croatian Serbs' fear to the Serbian narratives about Jasenovac having been calculated to make them feel afraid [29: 349/368; 116: 177–8]. Josip Glaurdić's recent assessment acknowledged that Tuđman confronted Milošević robustly, but argued that Tuđman's implicit claims to parts of Bosnia-Herzegovina impeded a united Croat/Bosniak front and increased support for Milošević among Croatian and Bosnian Serbs. He concluded Tuđman would have done better to reject the 'dangerous path' of 'play[ing] Milošević's game' [262: 86].

The future of the federation in 1990

After April–May 1990, one could say Yugoslavia's anti-Milošević bloc had two leaders: Kučan in Slovenia and Tuđman in Croatia. However, both republics had internal political divisions about what course to take, so their official actions were the result of political struggle and not simply individual decisions [171]. This is one reason why they often did not act in unity against Milošević. Another is that the Yugoslav national question had different implications for each republic. Of Slovenia's 1.97 million population, 1.73 million would identify themselves as Slovenes in 1992 [189: ix/xviii], and no territory in Slovenia was targeted by another nationalist programme within Yugoslavia. Croatia's 1981 population of 4.60 million, however, included 3.45 million Croats and 531,502 Serbs [22: 337; 29: 311]. By 1991 its population was counted at 4.78 million, including 3.74 million Croats, 581,663 Serbs, and a declining number of self-declared 'Yugoslavs' [29: 311; 85: 655]. The demographic differences are important for understanding the republics' actions in 1990–91 but did not pre-determine drawn-out war in Croatia. When reading about demographics, one should also remember that quoting national numbers and territorial majorities was itself a tool for achieving ethno-political aims during and after the break-up of Yugoslavia: the idea that belonging to an ethnic majority on the land would make people feel safe therefore needs to be questioned, not just assumed [48: 48].

The association between ethnic majorities, territory and security underlay the claims that Milošević and the SDS leader in Croatia, Jovan Rašković, made about Croatian Serbs' future in 1990. Both argued Croatian independence would violate the national self-determination of Croatian Serbs who did not want to live under sovereign Croatian rule. Milošević and his ally on the Yugoslav federal presidency, Borisav Jović, openly remarked about altering Croatia's borders to keep Croatian Serbs in Yugoslavia. Any Croatian intentions to secede would therefore have repercussions beyond Slovenia's own confrontation with the federal authorities. Tuđman's profile and policies compounded the tension, though any Croatian president would have encountered most of the same objections from Milošević and SDS [70: 216]. With these extra burdens, Croatia's government took longer than Slovenia's to commit to secession. Meanwhile, both republics made a joint proposal in October 1990 to drastically reform the Yugoslav federation along opposite lines to Milošević's.

The Slovenian–Croatian proposal envisaged Yugoslavia as a confederation of sovereign nation-states with their own defence and foreign policies, even the right to individually apply for European Community membership [262: 123]. This was potentially the last reasonable chance to preserve a Yugoslav state. Like the 1974 constitution and the 1989 constitutional amendments, it represents a touchstone moment for historians. Procedurally, it failed because Borisav Jović blocked it [29: 375]. Beyond this, there are varying views on whether it could have rescued Yugoslavia or whether it was even intended to succeed, with particular implications for the debate about Slovenian responsibility in 1990–91. Glaurdić argued the proposal reflected majority opinion in Slovenia and Croatia and that the Serbian leadership had already decided not to let it be considered, so responsibility for its failure lies with Milošević [262: 88]. Dejan Jović, conversely, considered the proposal a tactical step towards Slovenian and Croatian independence – and that neither leadership was fully committed to confederation in October 1990. He did emphasize, however, that Tuđman and Kučan aimed for independence 'without violence' [171: 251].

The confederal proposal appeared when Ante Marković was still ostensibly leading his own reform initiative. Marković had had the most to gain, yet lost the most, from multi-party elections. He began 1990 strongly: the 'shock therapy'-style reforms he introduced in January 1990, with US economists' advice, temporarily ended hyperinflation, and in spring 1990 opinion polls gave him 80 per cent support everywhere except Slovenia and Kosovo [38: 128–9]. He founded a party in July 1990, the Association of Reformist Forces of Yugoslavia (SRSJ), to contest republican elections, and launched a pan-Yugoslav broadcaster,

Yutel, from Sarajevo in October [21; 35: 34]. But Marković had started addressing the public too late to reach Slovenian and Croatian voters, who had already chosen different courses [160: 147]. By July, Yugoslav exports were already falling and more firms were going bankrupt. The economy worsened after August when Iraqi and Kuwaiti companies missed US$ 1 billion of payments to Yugoslav firms because of the Gulf War [262: 102]. Shock therapy's human costs now became apparent. The reforms weakened job protection but created no solutions for social security other than what the republics provided, and this strengthened republics' nationalist politicians, who could gain from blurring economic insecurities with ethno-national ones [11; 32; 38: 127].

By December 1990, every republic had governments opposing Marković's reforms [22: 357]. Slovenia and Croatia's elections had been in springtime. In November, a nationalist party reviving the name of the Internal Macedonian Revolutionary Organization (VMRO) won in Macedonia, while in Bosnia-Herzegovina – the very republic Marković most needed to carry [203: 161] – the three Bosniak, Croat and Serb parties won enough votes to govern as a coalition, though it is questionable whether this was ever intended to work (Chapter 4). Serbia's and Montenegro's elections in December both favoured Milošević. In Serbia, Milošević faced potential challenges both from non-Communist nationalist politicians and anti-authoritarian intellectuals [143]. The Serbian League of Communists, now the 'Socialist Party of Serbia' (SPS), could use former Party organizational structures plus Milošević's control over media. It comfortably defeated its nearest rival, the Serbian Renewal Movement (led by one of the 1980s nationalist novelists, Vuk Drašković) [146: 76–7]. These were essentially 'state-managed' elections, and Milošević then appropriated 18.2 billion dinars from the Yugoslav federal budget in order to fund public spending increases [24: 263; 262: 125]. The Montenegrin Party, led by Momir Bulatović, won Montenegro's elections and followed SPS by rebranding itself as the Democratic Party of Socialists.

The 1990 elections showed that Marković's project, not just his party, had failed. To keep Yugoslav politics federal, he needed to encourage other parties to build cross-republic alliances and create a genuinely pan-Yugoslav multi-party space [21; 38: 126]. But the successful parties in 1990 all formed and campaigned within individual republics. It was a great help to them, and a blow to

Marković, that the republics' elections all happened at different times [11: 67–8]. Many scholars argue the existing political crises had made cross-republic co-operation impossible. Those who blame Slovenia and Croatia for the break-up argue that, already set on independence, they financially weakened Yugoslavia by withholding federal taxes [17; 27]. Accounts holding Milošević primarily responsible argue he had quite simply made the federation untenable for Slovenia and Croatia by late 1990 [24; 25; 29; 134; 262]. Parallel to these short-term assessments is the longer-term view that the Party had already lost pan-Yugoslav legitimacy and only had legitimacy through leaders of particular republics [8: 72]. This position would use evidence from further back in Yugoslav history to explain why Marković did not succeed.

Most literature treats Marković as more of a supporting character than a protagonist. Indeed, neither Marković's new party nor any of the other non-nationalist political, intellectual and cultural movements that did arise in 1989–91 Yugoslavia have been much studied until recently [160; 181; 407]. The best-covered, but not only, such movement was the 'Association for a Yugoslav Democratic Initiative' (UJDI), founded by intellectuals in January 1989 [117]. The republican governments' nationalist policies and claims, including the effects of their interactions with each other, denied these alternatives political space to flourish. This was an actively-willed limiting of the political sphere [14; 21; 133], and the movements and ideas it excluded deserve to be better represented in the historical record. Forcing not only politics but everyday concerns to revolve around ethno-national belonging and threat became the central political dynamic of the Yugoslav wars.

Milošević, the JNA and the Croatian Serbs

Responsibility for whether Slovenian and Croatian independence would be peaceful or violent ultimately fell on the JNA, which held the predominant amount of equipment, arms and personnel within Yugoslavia. It could have refused to fulfil Milošević's objectives, but instead went along with them. Throughout Yugoslavia's lifetime, and especially when reformists were ascendant, the JNA had seen itself as existing to protect Yugoslav Communism against counter-revolution and subversion. The 1988 *Mladina* leaks had already shown the JNA weighing its options against the authorities of a republic that JNA commanders feared would bring down Yugoslavia; as insurance against decentralization, it had also reorganized its command structure in 1987 to prevent itself being easily divided into republican armies [230: 20]. Yet, since 1968, defence had not been solely a JNA matter. After the USSR invaded Czechoslovakia, Tito had introduced 'Territorial Defence' (TO), arming every municipality and large self-managing enterprise so that Yugoslavs could resist any future invader in a second Partisan uprising [161]. The JNA realized that republics' TOs could become nuclei for armed resistance, and secretly disarmed the Slovenian and Croatian TOs in May 1990 – but left the TOs of Croatian municipalities with Serb majorities alone [3: 48–9; 169: 534–5; 262: 89–91]. Both republics had to obtain weapons abroad, exercising an existing right to import arms but putting it to unintended purposes. Slovenia rearmed its TO and Croatia began militarizing its police. One arms deal by the Croatian Defence Minister, Martin Špegelj, was secretly filmed by the JNA. TV Belgrade broadcast it on the very evening in January 1991 when the federal Defence Minister, General Veljko Kadijević, was asking the federal presidency to forcibly disarm Croatia [34: 108–17; 35: 153–4].

The JNA/Milošević relationship in 1990–91 has been extremely well scrutinized. Key participants, including Kadijević and Borisav Jović, have both published (untranslated) memoirs relating to it [53: 108–25]. The International Criminal Tribunal for the Former Yugoslavia (ICTY) collected large amounts of evidence to establish the extent and timescale of Milošević's control over the JNA, essential in trying to prove that the war crimes they were investigating had a systematic nature (Chapter 7) [165: 22]. It is clear that the JNA developed a 'growing political bond' with Milošević during 1990, some argue as early as 1988 [176: 72–4]. Yet on occasions they were not in lockstep. In March 1991, when half a million people demonstrated against Milošević in Belgrade, Milošević and Jović planned to force a federal state-of-emergency declaration so that Kadijević could declare martial law – effectively a military coup. Kadijević did not follow through, either because the JNA had assessed it would not succeed or because he himself backed out from breaching the constitution [165: 56; 262: 142]. Afterwards, however, the JNA openly stood with Milošević and against the Croatian government on the Krajina question

[11: 402; 152: 323]. Even if it was not quite a 'de facto army of Serbia' [138: 151] by summer 1991 – Kadijević still disagreed with Milošević about strategy in autumn [4: 181–6] – its Serb composition rose from 40 per cent to 90 per cent by March 1992 as defections compounded deliberate Serbianization [165: 58]. Milošević also used the Serbian security services and paramilitary units as routes for covertly arming Serb Democratic Party militias and as alternative, unaccountable and personally-loyal instruments of force [4: 25–7; 165: 79–80].

Until 1990, Milošević had – publicly – stood for an authoritarian recentralization of Yugoslavia. By mid-1991, however, he favoured detaching the Serb-majority regions of Croatia and Bosnia-Herzegovina altogether. Had he always had nationalist objectives, and to what extent was his eventual objective to create a Greater Serbia by force? Even scholars who broadly agree about Milošević's historical role can disagree on some detail here: Hoare, Ramet, Glaurdić and Meier, for instance, all offer subtly different turning-points between January and December 1990 for Milošević's plans [26: 75/162; 29: 382; 134: 455; 262: 76]. Then there is the view in which Milošević was always engaged in the 'aggressive pursuit of Serb nationalism' and that his earlier recentralization agenda was only a feint [33: xvi]. These all emphasize premeditation. An alternative approach argues that Milošević changed policies opportunistically, whenever political and diplomatic conditions altered – as in 1990–91, and again later in the wars when he gave then withdrew support for Croatian/Bosnian Serb leaders [164: 282–3; 373: 341]. Readers must explore available sources on 1990–91 as closely as possible in assessing Milošević's war aims.

Another source of armed opposition to Croatia's independence (not Slovenia's) was the SDS militias in Krajina. For many Serbs in Krajina, the Croatian national symbols that were at the centre of Croatia's Statehood Day celebrations on 30 May 1990, then rolled out to Croatian institutions including the police, were symbols of genocide in 1941–45 not independence – family memories combining with arguments by revisionist intellectuals and the media in Serbia [112]. SDS told Serbs the Ustaša genocide risked being repeated if they allowed themselves to fall under Croatian rule [179]. On 25 July 1990, when the Croatian parliament amended the Croatian constitution to ban Cyrillic script outside Serb-majority areas, a newly-formed 'Serb National Council' announced a referendum on Serb autonomy. On 17 August, SDS militias blocked roads around Knin with logs, and JNA aircraft turned back three Croatian police helicopters that attempted to intervene [34: 100–1].

SDS and its para-state institutions remained strategically, militarily and economically dependent on Milošević's Serbia throughout the war in Croatia [28: 25–7; 173: 316–17]. However, it is over-simplistic to view them purely as puppets, nor was there one homogenous 'Croatian Serb' political position [157]. Firstly, although SDS existed before the April–May elections it performed poorly, as most Serbs voted for the ex-Communist SDP [34: 95]. Secondly, SDS went through an internal power struggle between Jovan Rašković, its founder in February 1990, and Milan Babić, the mayor of Knin who replaced Rašković as SDS leader that October. This rivalry helps show how the SDS leadership exerted power and knowingly brought about violence. Babić, unlike Rašković, could mobilize physical force, in co-operation with Milan Martić, the Knin police chief who had led the police resistance to Croatian state symbols [157: 625]. He could then intimidate residents and municipal councils in Serb-majority settlements that were still prepared to work with the Croatian authorities, so that co-operation broke off. Through this 'strategic' violence, Babić created a more homogenous territorial base for a rebellion [166: 29–30]. The autonomous municipalities declared themselves a 'Serb Autonomous Region of Krajina' (SAO Krajina) on 30 September 1990. Meanwhile, SDS began organizing in eastern Slavonia, where it would use the same strategy to take control of Serb-majority municipalities and hold them for the unified state Milošević was promising. Non-Serbs in these areas now had to fear the consequences of becoming a minority in a different ethnic state.

Armed conflict in Slovenia and Croatia

By spring 1991, Slovenia was moving towards independence with determination. In February, the republic declared its intention to secede, and in April passed the necessary laws and budget for functioning independently from Yugoslavia. It simultaneously prepared its Territorial Defence, intelligence service and elite police for action [3: 51–7]. The Slovenian Defence Minister, Janez Janša,

had been one of the *Mladina* journalists. Slovenia's likely secession tipped the balance of the Yugoslav federal presidency even
further away from Croatia, Bosnia-Herzegovina and Macedonia.
Milošević controlled the votes of Serbia, Montenegro, Kosovo
and Vojvodina, which until now had meant permanent deadlock.
Without Slovenia's vote, Milošević would have an institutionalized
majority. In February, the Bosnian and Macedonian Presidents,
Alija Izetbegović and Kiro Gligorov, proposed a new 'asymmetric'
federation where the Milošević republics could be tightly associated and Slovenia and Croatia could be much more separate. It
did not suit any other leaders.

Secession was much riskier for Croatia than Slovenia in spring
1991 because of the Croatian authorities' escalating conflict
with SDS. Tuđman was therefore slower to commit to independence than Kučan and Peterle: Slovenia held its independence
referendum on 23 December 1990 but Croatia only on 19 May
1991. Meanwhile, the Croatia/SDS conflict had escalated, with
the JNA consistently backing SDS. On 1 March 1991, the JNA
tried to prevent Croatian police re-establishing their authority in
Pakrac (western Slavonia), where SDS had instigated a rebellion
by Serb police. Another confrontation on 31 March in the Plitvice
Lakes National Park, which SDS wanted to incorporate into SAO
Krajina, marked the first deaths – one apiece – on each side. For
two weeks in April–May 1991 the JNA effectively besieged a Croat-
majority village, Kijevo, near Knin. Most serious were the killings
on 2 May at Borovo Selo, a suburb of Vukovar in eastern Slavonia.
Here, an SDS militia killed 12 Croatian police, leaving gruesome
images that shocked the Croatian public when broadcast. Borovo
Selo was a turning-point for Croatia's commitment to independence, for Croatian public opinion, and for most Croatian media
[34: 142–3]. In Croatia's independence referendum on 19 May,
93.2 per cent of participants voted to leave Yugoslavia – though
SAO Krajina boycotted the referendum, held its own, and
reported a 99 per cent vote to stay [70: 222]. With public man-
dates for secession, Croatia and Slovenia jointly declared independence on 25 June and began guarding their own borders. The
JNA mobilized to prevent their secession.

On 26–27 June 1991, the JNA intervened to retake the Slovenian
border-posts, and Slovenia's war of independence began [3: 59].
The JNA operation has been explained several ways: a reaction

to 'general confusion over appropriate action' among the federal presidency [38: 167]; a precedent premeditated by Milošević for JNA intervention in Croatia and Bosnia-Herzegovina [29: 393]; and, problematically for nostalgic interpretations of Ante Marković, the result of Marković ordering the JNA to re-establish federal authority over Slovenia's points of entry [26: 178; 262: 177]. Slovenia's soldiers were now doing exactly what Yugoslav defence ideology had prepared them for: resisting a more powerful invader in the forests [165: 226; 169: 529]. Eight Slovenian soldiers, 44 JNA soldiers and 15 civilians were killed during the next ten days [3: 68]. JNA operations against Slovenia ceased on 3 July as European Community negotiators sought a moratorium on independence. This agreement, signed at Brioni on 7 July, was supposed to delay Slovenian and Croatian secession for three months while the EC determined the Yugoslav republics' status under international law.

The Milošević–Jović plan for the JNA to attack Croatia so that SAO Krajina could enlarge itself – including by displacing non-Serbs from its territory – could now begin: the larger SAO Krajina became, the more land could eventually be incorporated into Serbia. If Milošević and Jović had 'no political commitment' to keeping Slovenia in Yugoslavia and wished to avoid overstretching the JNA before its offensives in Croatia, this would explain why the JNA followed a limited plan in Slovenia rather than its reserve plan of 'full mobilization' against Slovenian secession [165: 145–6]. The JNA began advancing into Croatia on 3–5 July 1991, first in eastern Slavonia, then opening a second front in Krajina. Paramilitary units recruited in Serbia, notably Željko Ražnatović-Arkan's group, joined the attack. The offensives forced non-Serbs out of the territory that was put under Krajina control and destroyed some settlements, such as Kijevo, altogether. The Dalmatian coast became another frontline, under JNA naval bombardment, and reserve units from Montenegro began attacking Dubrovnik, in the far south of Croatia, on 23 September. The heaviest Croatian losses were at Vukovar, which the JNA had encircled in late July and begun attacking in late August with reinforcements by Serbian paramilitary volunteers [4: 191–208]. When the JNA captured Vukovar on 18 November, 600 Croatian soldiers were killed, others detained in camps, and 264 soldiers and civilians taken from Vukovar hospital to a nearby farm to be shot [312: 1933].

The Krajina and Slavonia offensives followed a typical pattern, where SDS police and volunteers began operations and the JNA entered with artillery and armoured vehicles. They forced out civilians as well as soldiers, and looted or burned Croats' property so that they would not return. In early October, the JNA came within 20 km of Zagreb. The intimidating effects of this strategy were intended to spread along the JNA's future lines of advance. The attackers targeted homes, businesses, and historic and religious buildings that had marked the presence of anyone other than Serbs. The Krajina authorities consolidated their demographic claim further by resettling Serb refugees in Croats' empty homes. Some 84,000 Croats were displaced from SDS-controlled territories, which declared themselves the 'Republic of Serb Krajina' (RSK) on 19 December 1991.

The Croatian state did not fight back immediately. Some reasons were military: the National Guard (ZNG) it had started forming in April–May 1991 was not large or well-trained enough until late August. Politically, Tuđman had initially preferred to await Western support for Croatian independence, though the Croatian Army's Chief of Staff, Anton Tus, would have preferred offensive military action earlier [184; 262: 195]. The ZNG finally went into action on 14 September, blockading JNA barracks and depots in Croatia [4: 101–8]. The arms and equipment it confiscated greatly strengthened the Croatian arsenal. By this point, however, many semi-autonomous units had emerged that needed bringing under state command and control. The group that gained most from Tuđman's delaying tactics was the Croatian Party of Right (HSP), a far-right rival to HDZ, which organized its own paramilitary group, the Croatian Defence Forces (HOS). HOS presented their fighters as powerful and ready to attack, and consciously echoed NDH uniforms and symbols. Not only paramilitary groups but also some soldiers in the regular Croatian Army committed violent acts against Serb civilians which made Serbs living throughout Croatia feel unsafe and weakened Croatia's standing internationally. During the Croatian offensive to retake Gospić in October 1991, for instance, almost 100 Serb civilians were abducted and killed [70: 229]. Paramilitaries killed three members of the Zec family, who were Serbs, in Zagreb that December. In the months before the siege of Vukovar, more than

100 Serbs were abducted and tortured there, and other Serbs' houses were shot at, as an act of intimidation [312: 1942].

The first and most intense phase of the Croatian war of independence ended when the Croatian government and JNA signed a ceasefire in Sarajevo on 2 January 1992 (the 'Sarajevo Ceasefire', or the 'Vance Plan' after the UN Special Envoy Cyrus Vance). Špegelj would later criticize Tuđman for signing this at a moment of strength, implying Tuđman did this in order to use Croatian troops in Bosnia-Herzegovina [182: 35]. Within Croatia, the ceasefire remained controversial [185]. Abroad, however, the most sustained controversy concerns Croatia's and Slovenia's international diplomatic recognition later in January. The disputes surround, firstly, Germany's role, and secondly, the decisions of a European Community (EC) legal commission (the 'Badinter Commission') formed in autumn 1991 to advise which Yugoslav republics could be recognized. Germany has often been seen as decisively steering the EC towards recognizing Slovenia and Croatia, either as a principled liberal move [259] or, more critically, as a hasty measure that exacerbated the Yugoslav conflict [11: 51–3; 19: 75; 38: 183–9; 69: 211; 260; 261; 270: 29–32]. The Badinter Commission is part of the recognition controversy because it concluded that Slovenia and Macedonia could be recognized, whereas Croatia's provisions for Serb minority rights did not yet fulfil necessary criteria; the EC then recognized Slovenia and Croatia, but not Macedonia. Its critics mostly argue the recognition was too fast [17: 87–8; 27: 150; 269; 270: 28], though one found it too slow [2: 245]. Glaurdić's archival re-examination countered the anti-German positions, argued that Badinter's reservations about Croatia were based on a technicality that had been resolved in practice by January 1992, and criticized the EC, Britain, France and the USA for publicly insisting Yugoslavia stay together even once intelligence in mid-1990 suggested Milošević's policies would lead to war [45; 262].

Debating Croatian and Slovenian nationalism

The Croatian and Slovenian states both took steps to strengthen their national identities during and after their wars of independence. Because Croatia remained at war with the RSK and JNA until 1995 (Chapter 4), Croatian nationalism received particular scholarly attention [39; 187; 188; 199; 201]. 1990s Croatian nationalism was based on (re)joining Europe, building democracy, and expressing Croats' own historic culture, though as with any national identity, two points about nationalism complicated this description. Firstly, the content of Croatian national identity was not fixed, and interest-groups engaged in constant struggles to define it [154; 187; 188]. Istrian regionalists, for instance, contended Istria's history of multi-ethnic hybridity could make Croatian identity more pluralistic than Tuđman's ethno-centric version [186]. Moreover, Croatian national identity (like any other) depended on ideas about what Croatia *was not* as well as what Croatia *was* [199]. In 1990s Croatia, until Tuđman's death in December 1999, joining Europe implied rejecting 'the Balkans'; building democracy implied forgetting Yugoslavia and Communism; expressing Croats' historic culture meant rejecting anything to do with Serbs. These ideas had already existed in Croatian nationalism, but during the war could be turned into 'common sense'.

The attempt to separate Croatia from any kind of 'eastern', 'Balkan', 'Yugoslav' or 'Serb' culture affected language, popular culture and all areas of everyday life (Chapter 8). Many Communist street-names were changed to commemorate Croatian national heroes, though Tito usually remained. In 1994, Croatia renamed its currency the 'kuna' instead of the (Yugoslav) 'dinar'. 'Kuna' originated from a currency in the medieval Croatian kingdom, but the NDH had also used it. The name therefore became important in assessing Tuđman's attitudes to the NDH. Was it an overt attempt to embed 'Nazi heritage' in everyday life [190: 41–2]? Was it a centuries-old legacy that, logically, any sovereign Croatian state should reintroduce [26: 134; 158: 192]? Was it a symbol of the national reconciliation between former Communists and former Ustaše that Tuđman wanted to bring about [113: 137–8; 188: 106–7]? Renaming the currency was one of many early-1990s steps that distanced Croatia from Yugoslavia and Serbness. Whether the reader considers that this level of separation amounted to ethnic 'purification' depends on their beliefs about the rights and responsibilities of majority nations within a state.

Croatia's media were heavily involved in building and communicating the official narrative of national identity. They have become a frequent case-study for research into nationalism, the media and war, sometimes with reference to Croatia alone and sometimes in comparative studies also covering Serbia and/or Bosnia. The media played important roles in the Yugoslav wars. Some scholars see them as directly mobilizing people to support ethno-national separation [21; 35] while others argue that the media demobilized people by taking away space for political alternatives [14; 133]. Media could even be said to have generated ethnic identification and separation themselves rather than simply reflecting boundaries that already existed [39]. Messages about the national self and the enemy usually involved a neo-traditional ideology of gender, blending representations of innocent and defenceless women with representations of the national landscape, while praising men's heroic fighting strength [178]. Women's participation in actual political life was meanwhile declining, and reproductive rights were threatened in the name of increasing the national birth-rate [174; 196].

Sovereign Slovenia also used state media for nation-building. In 1990, the Ljubljana studio of Yugoslav Radio–Television had become Slovenia's national broadcaster (as had TV Zagreb in Croatia), promoting a unique Slovenian culture and history through its programming [202]. Slovenian national identity, also like Croatia's, emphasized that Slovenia belonged in a Europe that was separate from the Balkans [195]. But post-Yugoslav national identities were based on 'nesting' stereotypes, and from many Slovenian viewpoints Croatia was just as much part of the Balkans as Serbia or Bosnia were [108; 391]. Slovenia's citizenship laws also created a distinctive problem about who belonged to the nation. The laws envisaged an ethnic nation of Slovenes with other inhabitants of Yugoslavia as minorities. As many as 18,000 non-Slovenes, including 2,000 Roma, ended up without official residency rights and vulnerable to police harassment. Terming themselves 'the erased', they began campaigning for citizenship in 2002 [192]. The European Court of Human Rights upheld their case in 2012.

In Croatia, Slovenia and all other ex-Yugoslav republics, nationalism replaced Communism as the dominant ideology in public life. One common Western explanation was that the end of the Cold War had created an insecure vacuum where a 'new nationalism', authoritarian and ethnic, could flourish [2; 170].

Alternatively, post-Yugoslav nationalisms have been seen as results of deliberate strategies which coerced people into identifying as members of particular ethnic communities [14; 39]. Nationalism was not a force of nature; it was a human invention which could be traced back to a particular historical moment in late modern Europe and North America. As such, the conscious element in constructing and redefining national identities deserves to be made visible. Before and during the Yugoslav wars, this element was not just conscious but forcible, as becomes even clearer when turning to the outbreak and course of war in Bosnia-Herzegovina.

4 The War in Bosnia-Herzegovina

Open war in Bosnia-Herzegovina could be said to have begun on 31 March 1992, when the Yugoslav People's Army (JNA), Serb Democratic Party (SDS) authorities and paramilitary volunteers began attacking towns they envisaged as part of a Serb nation-state. Since September 1991, the Bosnian SDS had been declaring 'Serb Autonomous Regions' and trying to link them into a 'Republika Srpska' ('Serb Republic') in order to prevent the republic of Bosnia-Herzegovina being able to secede with all the territory inside its borders. The JNA had regrouped in Bosnia-Herzegovina after the Sarajevo Ceasefire with Croatia and could render the Bosnian the same support it had given Milan Babić's party. The Sarajevo government faced a similar threat in April 1992 to what the government in Zagreb had faced in June 1991, but the Croatian government's own territorial ambitions in Bosnia-Herzegovina put BiH and its people in an even more dangerous, isolated position. The war in Bosnia-Herzegovina lasted until December 1995, by which time 100,000 people had been killed and more than a million forced from their homes. It also became notorious as a conflict in which international diplomatic and peacekeeping interventions had failed to prevent genocide. The capture of Srebrenica by the Army of Republika Srpska (VRS) in July 1995, when paramilitaries and VRS soldiers killed 8,000 non-Serb men and boys, symbolizes this failure. Understanding the causes and duration of the Bosnian conflict requires appreciating Bosnia-Herzegovina's specific history through long-term and short-term lenses.

Ethnic identity and religion

Many accounts of the Bosnian conflict begin with Bosnia's long-term ethnic and religious history, in which each main ethnic category was associated with a different religious heritage: Croat identity with Catholicism, Serb identity with the Serbian Orthodox Church, and Muslim or Bosniak identity with post-Ottoman Islam. However, some interpretations emphasize ethno-religious divisions and violence; others emphasize inter-ethnic, inter-religious tolerance and coexistence; and some discuss active practices of identification rather than treating identity as a fixed characteristic. The first two approaches especially can lead to very different explanations for the 1992–95 war.

In 1992, the explanations most widely available in the West were those suggesting, like Misha Glenny, that Bosnia-Herzegovina's ethnic mixture would inevitably lead to violence without a larger state's 'protective shield' [16: 144]. Western politicians with power to affect policy towards former Yugoslavia spoke even more simplistically: for instance, the British Prime Minister, John Major, famously mentioned Bosnia's 'ancient hatreds' after the London Peace Conference on 26–27 August 1992 [1: 2]. Two books positing a post-Cold War resurgence of ethnicity and religion in international politics, Robert Kaplan's *Balkan Ghosts* and Samuel Huntington's *The Clash of Civilizations*, are often named as supporting this framework. They amplified it but did not create it: for instance, Douglas Hurd, the British Foreign Secretary, had already referred, in colonialist language, to the resurgent 'instinct to drive people of a different tribe out of your village' during a BBC interview about Yugoslavia in June 1991 [262: 176; 266].

Some other works in 1994–96 challenged the 'ethnic war' narrative by describing a country of ethnic and religious pluralism, epitomized by multi-confessional Sarajevo. They implied that, without external pressure, ethnic and religious differences had not mattered much to most Bosnians. Robert Donia and John Fine went furthest in stating that 'religious rivalry and violence were not [...] part of Bosnia's heritage' and that Bosnia had not experienced them 'before our own vicious twentieth century', during wars imported from Germany, Serbia and Croatia [223: 11–12]. They, and Rusmir Mahmutćehajić, argued Western governments had betrayed a tolerant Bosnian tradition [223; 240]. Noel Malcolm found the 'harmony' narrative overstated but agreed that Bosnia had a history distinct from Croatia or Serbia and needed to be preserved [241: xxi]. He, too, aimed to convince Western diplomats they should defend Bosnia's independence [46: 472–3]. The risk Bosnia-Herzegovina could be partitioned between Serbia and Croatia, with Western acquiescence, added urgency to these historians' defence of the 'tradition of tolerance and coexistence' which they saw the wartime Bosnian government as representing [223: 6–7]. Views of Bosnia 'as an organic and historic whole' or a separable 'purely artificial creation' [240: xiii] had very different policy implications, and it is no wonder the question was hard-fought [1: 323].

Microhistories of interpersonal conflict resolution add nuance to the antagonism/coexistence debate. Tone Bringa's anthropological study of Islam in a pre-war central Bosnian village suggested Bosnians did notice each other's ethno-religious identities but 'cultural pluralism was intrinsic' in society [212: 83]. Max Bergholz argued that ethnic antagonism was not part of 'most [Bosnian] people's everyday lives' post-1945 but suspicious incidents easily triggered it [59: 701–2]. Recent works on Sarajevo continued to weigh this balance [71; 222; 238; 334; 345]. Meanwhile, other studies on the dynamics of violence in 1992–95 and the politics of media, maps and censuses argued that ethnic identity was a conscious social construction in the present, aiming to show how processes of ethnic identification and categorization unfolded [14; 37; 48; 215; 252].

Could Bosnian history, however, be explained solely through histories of inter-ethnic relations? For one thing, to read it only as 'the supposed history of a conflict between nationalities' obscured the equally-significant question of divisions *within* national groups [76: 3]. Similarly, reading 1992–95 solely as a religious war could detract from historicizing the actual activities of clergy and religious institutions [28: viii–ix; 253]. Finally, the 'ethnic and religious' frame masked questions about the distribution of economic resources. Competition between, and within, nationalist political elites to appropriate the collapsed Yugoslav state's assets and infrastructure was a major factor in the wars [308; 342], and wartime logistics and recruitment were interdependent with organized crime [139; 183; 204; 226]. However, there is still no book-length history of organized crime in Bosnia-Herzegovina, let alone for the wars as a whole – a striking omission in the history of the conflict's short-term causes.

Nationalist politics and the outbreak of war

Three different nationalist parties won Bosnia-Herzegovina's elections in November 1990, forming a coalition. Alija Izetbegović's Party of Democratic Action (SDA), representing Muslim/Bosniak nationalism, won 36 per cent of seats in the Bosnian parliament. Radovan Karadžić's SDS won 30 per cent, and Stjepan Kljuić's Croatian Democratic Union (HDZ) won 18 per cent [203: 189]. These parties also won all seats on the new Bosnian collective presidency. None, however, could govern alone. Their national programmes implied other Yugoslav peoples would be their rivals and enemies. Yet they had a common interest in framing politics through the lens of ethno-national interests, and as a coalition they could avoid sharing power with parties that interpreted politics differently [221: 53]. No parliamentary alliances between alternative parties and 'moderate' nationalists were forthcoming [213: 13]. The three parties could force every political issue to be discussed in primarily ethno-national ways even while individually preparing themselves and their publics for more antagonistic relations later on.

The foundings of the Bosnian SDS and HDZ were closely linked to events in Croatia. The Bosnian SDS was founded in July 1990, and Karadžić's election campaigning frequently referred to the Croatian Krajina crisis and Serbs' right not to be left as minorities in other states. The Bosnian HDZ (HDZ BiH), meanwhile, started as a network of branches of Tuđman's party, holding its first separate congress in August 1990. HDZ BiH was internally divided on whether to seek autonomy within Bosnia-Herzegovina (Kljuić's position) or to undo Bosnia's existing borders and seek full union with Croatia (which a faction from western Herzegovina preferred). SDA, the Bosniak nationalist party founded in March 1990, also had a weighty choice: should it strive to recreate Bosnia-Herzegovina as a nation-state primarily governed by and for Bosniaks, or to promote a fully multi-ethnic Bosnia based on a historical narrative of coexistence and mixture? Izetbegović had written a religious nationalist declaration in 1970 for which he was imprisoned in 1983 [69: 192–6], though by 1990 he acted as a moderator between religious nationalism and multi-ethnic secularism. An early split in SDA showed these two national programmes sat uncomfortably together: in 1990, an SDA co-founder,

Adil Zulfikarpašić, left, alarmed by the religious imagery in Izetbegović's campaign [28: 77/87/142].

In 1991, the coalition partners ostensibly shared power but each prepared to defend their separate interests. Cabinet decisions could be easily deadlocked, especially on defence and security [230: 22]. SDS obstructionism slowed down parliament, while in local government the nationalist parties often failed to agree power-sharing measures [84: 194; 203: 192–6]. Parliamentary co-operation broke down as the conflict in Croatia intensified, with a 'final split' over whether to obstruct JNA operations in Croatia [3: 125]. Yet recent research using sources outside party politics suggests the Bosnian public exhibited much more support for anti-war initiatives than political elites did [181]. This, again, invites consideration of what prevented these movements mobilizing as alternative forces in official politics.

Each nationalist party meanwhile arranged access to arms, using municipal Territorial Defence caches where possible [230]. HDZ BiH organized autonomous local militias which came together as the 'Croat Defence Council' (HVO) in April 1992. The SDA started obtaining arms in December 1990 and formed its own military organization, the 'Patriotic League', in July 1991. SDS also formed militias and started connecting municipalities on the Croatian Krajina pattern, in a so-called 'regionalization' process (linking municipalities into one entity) [221: 76–81]. It declared four 'Serb Autonomous Regions' in September 1991: Bosanska Krajina (including Banja Luka and Prijedor), North-Eastern Bosnia (including Bijeljina), Herzegovina (including Trebinje), and 'Romanija' (including an outlying part of Sarajevo, Pale) [252: 107–8]. SDS knew it could also rely on JNA arms, equipment and personnel in campaigning to detach the 'Autonomous Regions' from the Sarajevo government [3: 129–30; 221: 94–7]. Indeed, in September 1991 the JNA took its first actions in Bosnia-Herzegovina against armed Bosniaks and Croats who were trying to stop JNA troops and equipment moving towards Croatia [29: 416].

SDS left the Bosnian parliament on 15 October 1991, after Karadžić gave a speech threatening Bosniaks might 'disappear' in case of war [221: 118]. It formed a Serb assembly on 24 October, held a referendum two weeks later on seceding as the 'Autonomous Region of Krajina' (ARK), and proclaimed a sovereign 'Republika

Srpska' on 9 January 1992. Behind the scenes, on 19 December 1991 it sent key members instructions for setting up 'crisis head-quarters' or 'crisis staffs' (*krizni štabovi*) during an emergency: in spring 1992, these organizations would manage Republika Srpska's political and military takeover of territory and its persecution of non-Serbs. The 'crisis headquarters' document is important evidence in arguments that the SDS takeover was pre-planned [165: 122; 206: 58–61; 221: 121].

To fulfil EC conditions for recognizing Bosnia-Herzegovina, Izetbegović called an independence referendum for 29 February–1 March 1992. SDS ensured as many Serbs as possible boycotted the referendum in areas it controlled. Sixty three per cent of all registered voters, and 99.7 per cent of participants, still voted for Bosnian independence [29: 417; 213: 117]. Some fighting for control over territory began in March. In Sarajevo, after the Bosniak gangster Ramiz Delalić-Ćelo shot dead a member of a Serb wedding party on 1 March, SDS members barricaded several streets, beginning the competition for urban space that would develop into the outright besieging and division of the city [221: 162–5]. In Mostar, Bosanski Brod and other settlements in Herzegovina and Posavina, the HVO began fighting the JNA. On 31 March, paramilitary detachments and Serbian special police crossed the Serbian border into eastern Bosnia. They killed and expelled Muslims from Bijeljina, Zvornik and the other towns they entered in early April, and the JNA followed them to consolidate RS territorial control [34: 224; 165: 178–9; 206: 81–101]. Peace activists called a 100,000-strong peace demonstration in Sarajevo. The demonstration was broken up when SDS paramilitaries attacked the crowd on 5 April, but deserves to be taken seriously as evidence of public demands for Bosnian leaders to reach an agreement [21: 99; 34: 226–8; 243]. Bosnia-Herzegovina declared independence the next day [262: 297].

Ethno-political violence and 'ethnic cleansing'

Throughout the Bosnian conflict, the VRS, which was officially split from the JNA on 4 May 1992, used violence and terror against civilians to conquer territory, join it into one contiguous entity, remove people identified as enemy minorities from the land, and establish new state structures that could eventually unify with Serbia. Radovan Karadžić, addressing the RS parliament on 12 May 1992, set out its territorial programme: separating Serbs from Croats and Bosniaks, and creating a contiguous, defensible and economically-viable territory for the Serbs. Now known as Karadžić's 'six strategic goals' speech, this has joined the December 1991 'crisis headquarters' document as evidence that the top-level RS leadership planned to remove non-Serbs [4: 4–5; 206: 66–7; 221: 203–7; 252: 5]. Facing this threat, the Sarajevo government had to combine various armed units, including the SDA's Patriotic League and any pro-Sarajevo Territorial Defence elements, into the Army of the Republic of Bosnia-Herzegovina (ARBiH). This fought to defend Bosnia-Herzegovina's territorial integrity and sovereignty. The HVO, though initially allied with the Bosnian government, also aspired to create its own territorial entity ('Herceg-Bosna') to unify with Croatia. HDZ BiH used paramilitaries as well as the HVO to fulfil these aims, and pursued them by killing, imprisoning and removing non-Croats. The Croatian government was long rumoured to be implicated in this strategy, and the mid-2000s revealed a 'parallel chain of command' between the Croatian HDZ and irregular Croat units in Bosnia-Herzegovina [374: 453].

Narrating the Bosnian war as a triangular conflict between three ethnic nations would nonetheless miss important points about each side's aims and composition – and about the power imbalance that disadvantaged the underequipped, isolated Sarajevo government throughout the war. Ethnic identity, firstly, did not always predetermine what side someone took. Fikret Abdić, ex-director of Agrokomerc, was a Bosniak but fought against the ARBiH to claim personal authority over the Bihać area. Thousands of Serbs remained in Sarajevo rather than moving to RS territory, and some (such as the karate-champion-turned-policeman Dragan Vikić or the ex-JNA general Jovan Divjak) held important roles in defence. A young Serb from Trebinje, Srđan Aleksić, who defended a Croat friend from RS police at the cost of his own life in January 1993, became a figure for pacifist commemoration after the wars.

Another problem with the 'ethnic triangle' approach is that the ARBiH was not conceived as solely Bosniak; it was first devised as a genuinely multi-ethnic force. In 1994–95 it did take on openly-Bosniak nationalist ideology and make increasing use of religious, Islamic symbolism, but this only came after a protracted political struggle over how closely to identify it with SDA [220; 230: 101–7]. Finally, foreign states' diplomatic and military decisions also affected the conflict. The Bosnian war can be called ethno-political insofar as the participants' aims (even at certain times the Sarajevo government's) related to exerting power over territory in the name of an ethnically-defined nation, but this is far from being 'ethnic' violence in the sense of automatically arising because of ethnic differences.

The war in Bosnia-Herzegovina, as in Croatia, revolved around taking control of inhabitants and buildings in populated areas. This 'micro' level means scholars can best understand its dynamics through detailed study of particular localities. The takeover of the Prijedor area (north-west Bosnia) in May 1992 is often used to illustrate what happened [4: 305–6; 221: 200–3; 228; 255]. On 30 April 1992, an SDS militia, supported by the JNA and paramilitaries from Serbia, entered Prijedor and began making it part of Republika Srpska. Over the next month they abducted non-Serb cultural and political leaders and took them to nearby prison camps, then rounded up non-Serb men in general. Simultaneously, they took over large businesses and public services, including Prijedor hospital, and dismissed non-Serbs, as well as Serbs they considered politically suspect. The RS forces then pushed out into nearby villages where Bosniaks and Croats lived. They killed some inhabitants at once, subjected the survivors to torture and sexualized violence in detention, then expelled them to central Bosnia [228: 68–70]. Serb refugees from other parts of Bosnia-Herzegovina settled in the empty homes.

The political and military strategy of ethno-political violence during the Yugoslav wars has often popularly been called 'ethnic cleansing', a term from the local language(s) (*etničko čišćenje*) which foreign war reporters introduced into English. Suspicion that the term has been used euphemistically to deflect attention from genocide has since made it problematic [163]. That said, it can still be used while recognizing genocide: Hariz Halilovich, for instance, called the genocidal killings at Srebrenica 'the logical extension of the [RS authorities'] policy of ethnic cleansing' [228]. Gow defined ethnic cleansing as 'the strategic use of excessive violence against civilian population centers, demonstrative atrocity and mass murder in order to remove that population [...] to secure the territory in question' [165: 118–9]. His reference to 'demonstrative' atrocity emphasized that ethno-political violence had an integral symbolic dimension, unmaking communities' past as well as their present through violence [156; 228]. The desired result was to alter people's own understandings of the past so that they remembered 'them' having always hated 'us' [345: 13].

Perpetrators of ethno-political violence desecrated many religious buildings, including an estimated 1,000–1,100 mosques, 340 Orthodox churches and monasteries and 450 Catholic sites [248; 253: 260–1]. They also targeted symbols of historic coexistence, such as Mostar's Old Bridge, which the HVO demolished on 9 November 1993. Even direct bodily attacks could be symbolic. Serb troops sometimes made Muslim prisoners eat pork; survivors from several camps reported being forced to sing their captors' or own people's national songs while being tortured [411]. The form of abuse that has been most discussed is sexualized violence against women (much less has been said about sexualized violence against men). VRS camp guards at Foča, in eastern Bosnia, organized the systematic rape of non-Serb women by Serb men [355]. Women were also raped in other camps, and when soldiers were evicting civilians. More than in any previous conflict, wartime rape became an international issue during the Bosnian war. One group of Croatian feminists contended that Serb rapes of non-Serb women in Croatia and Bosnia were a deliberate plan to exterminate the next generation of Croats and Muslims. Nationalist movements, including some feminists, then competed over each nation's number of raped women, while in the West the radical feminist Catharine MacKinnon wrote about wartime rape in Bosnia as part of her arguments against pornography [239]. Edina Bećirević integrated MacKinnon's argument about 'genocidal rape' into her narrative of RS attacks on Bosniaks [206: 123].

While graphic accounts of war rape multiplied in English [250], anti-nationalist feminists in Croatia and Serbia rejected the argument that Serbs were more inclined to rape than other nations. Instead, they argued patriarchy, misogyny and militarism in general were what caused rape in war [51; 236]. This was an important corrective to the simplistic narratives that dominated popular understandings of what was happening in Bosnia. Recent reassessments of the 1990s arguments about wartime rape expand their analyses by thinking further about how gender and ethno-nationalism intersected. Dubravka Žarkov noted that, while women were paraded as symbolic victims, sexualized attacks against men were rarely discussed because the very idea men could be raped undermined nationalist associations between masculinity and power [39: 155–69]. Elissa Helms observed that nearly all literature on wartime rape in Bosnia came from outside Bosnia and much involved stereotypical assumptions about rural communities and Islam. When writers instrumentalized wartime rape to advance ideological aims, survivors' own voices went unheard [318].

Any history of the Yugoslav wars needs to acknowledge that ethno-political violence in Bosnia-Herzegovina caused 'the near-total unmixing of the population in terms of nationality' [327: 141]. However, explaining the violence as an inevitable result of 'ethnic incompatibility' was insufficient [215: 88–93; 257: 159]. Not only would that obscure intra-ethnic rivalries and impede awareness that ethnic identities could sometimes be ambiguous, but it would mask another important dimension: socio-economic competition and struggle. Wartime authorities monopolized employment and housing for their loyalists and denied it to their enemies, removing economic means as well as cultural and social means for victims to continue living there. In Banja Luka, for instance, the RS 'crisis headquarters' led by Radoslav Brđanin dismissed almost all non-Serb workers from banks, hospitals, schools and the university [224]. Political, military and criminal elites made huge gains from privatizing property and companies they confiscated from the state. The socio-economic dimensions of ethno-political violence during the Yugoslav wars still deserved more research, though research on the targeting of cities explored these dimensions to some extent.

Cities under siege

Foreign attention during the Bosnian war centred on the capital, Sarajevo. The VRS targeted Sarajevans with artillery bombardment from positions around the mountains, and sniper fire from apartment blocks in city districts it controlled. On 2 May 1992, the JNA tried to divide Sarajevo entirely, even temporarily capturing Izetbegović. Several different armed organizations – including the Territorial Defence (TO), HVO units, and organized criminal groups – mobilized 10–15,000 people in defence [230]. On 3 May, when the JNA retreated, TO soldiers fired on the convoy in Dobrovoljačka Street, killing seven JNA troops [34: 236–43]. The RS government considered this a war crime, whereas the Sarajevo government considered the convoy a military target. These incompatible positions continued to inform public narratives about the 'Dobrovoljačka incident' (and another similar case in Tuzla) after 1995 [337: 274–80].

After May 1992, the VRS siege continued. Snipers fired on civilians fetching water and supplies, and artillery targeted outdoor crowds. The three worst artillery attacks were the 'breadline massacre' in May 1992, which killed 18 people, and the attacks on the Markale marketplace in February 1994 and August 1995, which killed 68 and 37 people, respectively [233: 211–12; 267: 89]. The VRS turned Sarajevo's electricity, water and gas on and off at will, adding to inhabitants' sense of powerlessness. They also aimed to destroy historic and cultural institutions, including Sarajevo's library (the 'Vijećnica'), set alight by VRS incendiary shells on 25 August 1992. Sarajevans' prevailing public narratives of the siege remember resilience, resourcefulness and dark humour. Less comforting, thus less commemorated, are memories of moral compromise, whether this meant participating in the black market or compromising the cherished myth of multi-ethnic Sarajevo by giving in and viewing ethnic groups as the basic building-blocks of society [238; 334; 345].

In May 1993, the UN Security Council (UNSC) recognized Sarajevo as a 'safe area', along with five other towns the ARBiH had been holding against the VRS – Tuzla, Srebrenica, Goražde, Bihać and Žepa. The VRS controlled access to them and could cut off humanitarian relief. Although the six cities had encirclement in common, they also had different microhistories of war. Tuzla stood out as the only wartime Bosnian city which had non-nationalist leaders in power, and civic activists weathered several attempts by SDA to win support among local Bosniaks [205]. Bihać, meanwhile, not only defies easy explanations of the Bosnian war as an ethnic conflict but may also have been an underappreciated military turning-point [229]. In September 1993, Fikret Abdić declared his 'Autonomous Province of Western Bosnia' around Bihać and won over soldiers from several local

ARBiH brigades, including many ex-Agrokomerc employees. He made a pact with the VRS in October [213: 154]. The ARBiH launched offensives in autumn 1994 and spring 1995 to retake Bihać and break the Abdić–VRS alliance. By the end of the war, four of the six 'safe areas' were under ARBiH control and three (Tuzla, Goražde and Sarajevo) had continuously held out. However, the fate of the other two, Srebrenica and Žepa, would prove the UN's guarantee utterly illusory.

The wartime destruction of cities was more than material damage. It can be seen as a sustained campaign against enemies' cultural heritage and against historical evidence of a multi-ethnic, multi-confessional past [248]. It has even been called 'urbicide', attacking the very idea of cities as places where people coexist in diversity [11: 184; 218]. Even pre-war ex-Yugoslav urban identities had juxtaposed concepts of a cosmopolitan, modern city against traditionalist, uncivilized villages and highlands. During the wars, this cultural history led to a narrative of the conflicts as a 'revenge of the countryside' against the city. The rural family origins of Radovan Karadžić, presiding over the siege of Sarajevo from the hills, were a key image [210; 274: 78]. So was the VRS artillery attack on Tuzla's main square on 25 May 1995, killing 71 young people celebrating an ex-Yugoslav public holiday. A Serbian architect, Bogdan Bogdanović, famously described the attacks on Vukovar, Mostar and Sarajevo as a 'battle between city lovers and city haters' [209: 54]. In socio-economic terms, the economic deprivation of areas such as western Herzegovina, or Krajina in Croatia, contributed to resentment towards the metropolis and may have played into public support for nationalist parties in 1990 [106]. The anthropology of rural/urban relations during Yugoslav industrialization, however, suggested it was more productive to look at connections between countryside and city rather than separations between them [210; 347].

Foreign peace plans and the HVO/ARBiH war

Besides the war's internal dimensions, foreign diplomacy, journalism and peacekeeping also affected the Bosnian conflict. Indeed, even before the war foreign diplomats had started negotiating peace plans. The first, the 'Lisbon Agreement' or 'Cutileiro

Plan', was proposed in February–March 1992 as an EC attempt to avert war before the Bosnian referendum. It envisaged Bosnia-Herzegovina composed of more than a hundred 'cantons', small Swiss-style autonomous units each reflecting their population's majority ethno-national identity. The plan failed not just because Izetbegović changed his mind but because SDA, SDS and HDZ made competing claims about which areas should have which majorities [34: 219–20; 252: 151]. However, its basic principle – the idea of resolving the conflict through a territorial settlement based on mapping ethnic majorities – also informed the future peace plans [240: 38].

This idea, though supposedly a path to peace, was damaging. Firstly, accepting 'the ethnic principle' [262: 290] meant accepting the SDS–HDZ logic that ethnic groups should make themselves autonomous in areas where they had majorities. Moreover, the link between ethnic majority and territorial control became an inducement to consolidate territorial claims violently – especially, Glaurdić argued, for Republika Srpska, which had Serbia's support [262: 290–1]. This 'nexus between identity and territory' thus predated April–May 1992 [215: 129]. SDS and HDZ formalized it in a partition pact, the 'Graz Agreement', on 6 May 1992 [221: 145–6]. But Bosnia's ethnic geography could not accurately translate to units on a map. The Cutileiro plan would have left hundreds of thousands of people outside their allotted ethnic spaces and erased non-Bosniak/Croat/Serb identities from political significance [252: 150–1]. Later plans varied the number and composition of territorial units, yet the principle remained [215].

The August 1992 London Conference appointed new UN and EC representatives, Cyrus Vance and David Owen. The draft 'Vance–Owen Plan', published on 2 January 1993, proposed ten cantons with boundaries to be negotiated. Karadžić and the RS parliament rejected it for not creating one contiguous Serb entity, though Milošević had – genuinely or not – pressured them to sign it [376]. Vance–Owen also worsened relations between the Sarajevo government and the Bosnian Croat authorities. These were already shaky, as one HDZ faction's aspirations to create a separate Croat entity ('Herceg-Bosna') threatened a united Bosnia just as much as the RS's goals did. The leader of the Herceg-Bosna faction, Mate Boban, took over HDZ BiH in autumn 1992, and on 23 October 1992 the HVO forced up to

5,000 Bosniaks out of the town of Prozor [3: 159]. Boban felt empowered by Vance–Owen to establish sole authority over the supposed Croat cantons, and arguably to expel non-Croats from them [74: 379]. Vance–Owen's implication 'that the only real players are the ethno-religious communities' [11: 6] had both military and moral consequences.

After January 1993, the HVO/ARBiH conflict or 'Bosniak–Croat' conflict (depending on whether authors choose organizational or ethno-national terminology) became open warfare along a new frontline in Herzegovina and central Bosnia. An HVO assault detachment killed at least 103 Bosniak villagers in Ahmići on 16 April 1993 [4: 417–19]. The HVO siege of Mostar (May 1993–January 1994) split the city into 'Croat' and 'Bosniak' halves, which effectively outlasted the war [321]. The Sarajevo government called, unsuccessfully, for Mostar, Vitez and Maglaj to become UN Safe Areas [256: 101]. In November 1993, it also assimilated Sarajevo's HVO brigade into the ARBiH. This removed the risk of the HVO operating independently in Sarajevo and consolidated SDA control over armed forces on the government side, coming a few weeks after the disarming of two brigades commanded by gangsters (Ćelo and Mušan Topalović-Caco) who had fought alongside the government in 1992 [3: 186–7; 230: 98–100]. A US-sponsored ceasefire between the ARBiH and HVO on 1 March 1994 (the 'Washington Agreements') ended their armed conflict, but left a mistrustful legacy within the 'Federation of Bosnia-Herzegovina' that this agreement formed.

Scholars assessing the HVO/ARBiH conflict must explore whether the Croatian state and Tuđman were implicated in the attempted forcible creation of a mono-ethnic Bosnian Croat entity. During the International Criminal Tribunal for the Former Yugoslavia (ICTY) appeal of Tihomir Blaškić (the HVO colonel whose area of responsibility included Ahmići), evidence emerged about a parallel command structure between Zagreb and military units in Bosnia-Herzegovina [374: 453]. Beyond this, it was widely rumoured that Tuđman and Milošević met in March 1991, even as the Krajina conflict was escalating, to agree a future partition of Bosnia-Herzegovina [262: 150–3]. Donia even suggested Tuđman was 'receptive' to a January 1992 RS proposal to partition Bosnia-Herzegovina three ways and organize population transfers

[221: 144]. A hardline Herzegovinian faction within the Croatian HDZ influenced Tuđman's policy, though in aspiring to politically unify the Croats he might anyway have welcomed expanding the borders of the Croatian state.

A revised peace plan in August 1993 put Bosnia-Herzegovina at visible risk of partition. The 'Owen–Stoltenberg Plan' proposed dividing Bosnia-Herzegovina into three ethnic units, and in 1993's political–military context the Serb and Croat units could easily have seceded to join Serbia and Croatia. A remaining Bosniak entity might then not even have survived [216; 223; 240]. Abroad, partition was being recommended as the only solution the belligerents would accept or because Bosnia had already been partitioned in practice; in late 1993, a desperate Sarajevo government was reportedly considering accepting partition [216: 151–2; 240: 52–5] before its diplomatic and military situation improved in 1994, and SDA started intensifying mono-ethnic Bosniak nationalism [21]. From outside, the best hope for ending the war seemed to be strengthening United Nations intervention. Bosnians on the Sarajevo side, however, already had bitter reason to disbelieve UN guarantees.

Humanitarian intervention, peacekeeping and the media

Foreign powers' attitudes towards Bosnians' extensively-documented suffering haunted 1990s Western histories of the Yugoslav wars. The deployment of peacekeeping forces to former Yugoslavia was slow and hesitant. In February 1992, the UN sent 15,000 peacekeepers ('UNPROFOR') to Croatia to demilitarize the so-called 'UN Protected Areas' (mostly, the Republic of Serb Krajina (RSK)-controlled areas) and help refugees return. The troops could not stop expulsions, only report ceasefire violations [263: 102–4]. In September 1992, the UNSC mandated UNPROFOR to assist the UN High Commissioner for Refugees (UNHCR) in delivering humanitarian aid around Bosnia. Foreign military forces' mandate, size and role in Bosnia did gradually extend. The UNSC declared a 'no-fly zone' over Bosnia in October 1992 to prevent military flights, though local forces (especially the VRS) often broke it. It had no enforcement mechanism until March–April 1993, when NATO's 'Operation Deny Flight' was permitted to shoot down unauthorized aircraft.

This enforcement problem typified peacekeeping in Bosnia, which in Hoare's view 'hindered rather than helped Bosnian efforts at self-defense' [18: 127]. UNPROFOR could use force in self-defence but not intervene in atrocities such as Ahmići – and the mandate potentially gave non-interventionist generals and politicians a convenient excuse not to act on intelligence [273]. The UN Safe Areas, like the no-fly zone, initially lacked an enforcement mechanism too [256]. Recognizing this problem, a liberal critique of UN peacekeeping held that in Bosnia-Herzegovina, as in Rwanda, the UN and member states should have used force to prevent genocide [268; 271]. Wartime advocates of further intervention called for a 'lift and strike' policy – lifting the arms embargo to help the Sarajevo government, and using NATO air-strikes against the VRS [268: 302]. Opponents charged them with failing to accept the war's 'tragic new realities' [213: 187].

Both sides of the Western 'lift and strike' debate discussed the region's past. Brendan Simms, for instance, argued British officers who saw the conflict simply as between devious 'warring factions' failed to recognize VRS/HVO aggression against Bosniaks [273: 182]. By narrating Balkan history as inherently violent, Western soldiers and politicians could disavow any Western ethical responsibility for the war continuing. David Campbell, indeed, suggested their representations 'had more in common with the Serbian position than that of the Bosnian government' [215: 49], and Gregory Kent accused them of 'false balancing' [267: 252]. Pro-intervention arguments thus tried to reframe Bosnia as a site of genocide, arguing foreign states had a universal responsibility to prevent it [266: 109]. Some also used the language of 'appeasement' [2: 308; 274]. Meanwhile, prominent journalists emotively reported on civilian suffering as further pressure for more forceful intervention.

Bosnia entered journalistic history both for the immediate, intimate warzone reporting permitted by video technology, but also for inspiring a new model of journalistic ethics that abandoned traditional bystanders' objectivity [208; 225; 274]. The BBC's Martin Bell called this 'journalism of attachment' in explaining his reporting from Sarajevo [208: 138–45]. Media reports did not sway politicians towards intervention on their own – whatever the 'CNN effect' theory implied – but could force politicians to respond at specific moments [264]. In August 1992, for instance, several US and UK journalists visited VRS concentration camps at Omarska and Trnopolje near Prijedor [227; 254], and newspapers reusing the images likened the conditions to the Holocaust [214: 2–6; 216: 8–9]. Even then, however, it has been argued that Western governments, continuing to frame the conflict as a primarily humanitarian crisis, prolonged it by failing to protect civilians from violence [232: 176] or act on 'the genocidal character of the war against Bosnia' [267: 149].

Foreign media reports had more impact on non-governmental levels, inspiring foreign volunteers to visit and assist particular sides. This included activists from peace campaigns, trades unions and religious institutions who organized grassroots aid convoys [234], but also a few thousand mercenaries and volunteers who attached themselves to various sides as paramilitaries. These included the so-called 'Greek Volunteer Guard' (members of the far-right group Golden Dawn among them), which participated in the VRS attack on Srebrenica in July 1995, and the 300–3,000 foreign 'mujahidin' who considered they were defending a global Islamic community in Bosnia [235; 244]. With the exception of diaspora networks [168], there are very few studies of the humanitarian or military dimensions of foreign volunteering during the wars [150; 234].

Media could also influence foreign knowledge and policy through implicitly and explicitly explaining the war. Beyond arguments about whether Western media were inherently biased against Serbs [19: 116; 265; 270: 144], more productive analyses concern how the media viewed ethnicity itself. Like the foreign peace plans, media explanations for the wars often assumed ethnic difference and mixing inherently caused instability [257]. They fitted Bosnia into political and cultural geography ambiguously. Bosnia could be seen as a civilized 'heart of Europe', 'on the doorstep' of the West, but also placed in the 'primitive, barbarian [...] Balkans' where ancient ethnic hatreds reigned [272: 385–7]. One travel book, Kaplan's *Balkan Ghosts*, is often credited with persuading Clinton foreign intervention could not solve the Bosnian conflict [220: 168; 266: 150–5; 268: 302; 271: 256]. Kaplan was not even writing about Bosnia, but his depiction of historic mutual Serb–Croat brutality in the Croatia chapter supported discourses about specifically Balkan ancient hatreds. Glenny's *Fall of Yugoslavia* was suggested as a similar influence on some British politicians and generals [53: 82–3; 267: 349].

In August 1993, first steps towards 'lift and strike' emerged when UNPROFOR was allowed to use NATO Close Air Support for stopping artillery attacking the Safe Areas – although the arms embargo still existed. A drawn-out UN approval process, based more on diplomatic politics than strategic considerations within Bosnia, often made the air-strikes' power useless [247: 77–8]. UNPROFOR threatened air-strikes against VRS positions near Sarajevo after the February 1994 Markale massacre, and did call them in April 1994 against the VRS attack on Goražde [213: 147]. In response, the VRS commander Ratko Mladić ordered UNPROFOR troops taken hostage whenever air-strikes were used [263: 151–2]. This new strategy successfully intimidated the UN [221: 256–65]. After the largest hostage-taking (at Goražde) in May 1995, the UNSC gave UNPROFOR an extra 'Rapid Reaction Force', supposedly able to rescue UNPROFOR hostages or even evacuate the UN. However, none of these changes protected one UN Safe Area, Srebrenica, from the catastrophic VRS attack in July 1995.

Srebrenica and the recognition of genocide

Srebrenica was the worst and largest massacre in the Bosnian conflict, and the greatest failure of international peacekeeping in Bosnia-Herzegovina. VRS offensives in eastern Bosnia had targeted Srebrenica at once, but it had held out as an enclave under nominal UN protection. Srebrenica had accommodated thousands of Bosniak refugees from other settlements, and townspeople believed the Sarajevo government could have defended the area more strongly [247: 127]. On 8 July 1995, the VRS and paramilitaries began attacking Srebrenica. The plan is usually attributed to Mladić, though Donia now argues Karadžić had a 'primary role' [221: 250]. Soldiers took over several UNPROFOR observation-posts and separated out non-Serb townspeople. The UNPROFOR commander and UN special envoy in Bosnia-Herzegovina refused the Dutch UN battalion's request for air-strikes [74: 393]. The Dutch soldiers evacuated Srebrenica, taking a few locally-recruited employees with UN accreditation but leaving all others behind [231: 42–4]. On 11–13 July, the VRS and paramilitaries abducted the 8,000 remaining men and boys to nearby sites, where they shot them dead and left them in mass graves. The VRS captured nearby Žepa on 25 July, further consolidating RS power in eastern Bosnia.

The ICTY and the International Court of Justice have both ruled that the systematic killing at Srebrenica was genocide (international law makes intent to destroy an ethnic group *in part* sufficient for genocide convictions) (Chapter 7). Other ICTY trials acquitted defendants of genocide but convicted them of crimes with shorter sentences, apparently reasoning that the strategy of making a territory ethnically homogenous did not automatically imply mass extermination of a group [246: 26; 337: 115]. The forced displacement and persecution inherent in 'ethnic cleansing' strategies destroyed communities but did not, for those judges, constitute genocide. Scholars, too, must decide whether and how to mention 'genocide' when referring to Bosnia. Donia followed ICTY practice [221: 18]. Some others argued that any evidence of 'intentional group destruction' was sufficient for applying the term and, thus, if RS authorities in 1992 had already manifested the intent motivating the Srebrenica massacre, the VRS's whole strategic project could and should be termed genocide (or the Bosnian Genocide) [74: 353; 163: 303; 206: xiii; 216; 267: 8; 369: 1194]. Historians should be sensitive to these concerns, but should also beware of a point where demands for recognition of genocide turn into demands to recognize whole nations as collectively innocent or genocidal [246].

After 1995, Srebrenica became a site of memory inside and outside Bosnia-Herzegovina [337]. Annual commemorations at the Potočari memorial complex, including reburials of newly-identified victims, began in 2003. The commemoration was a national political event in the Federation of Bosnia-Herzegovina, though some survivors came to worry that Bosniak political and religious elites were appropriating their pain [228]. Bosnian Serb and Croat nationalists met Bosniak claims for genocide recognition with counter-claims that their own nations' suffering should equally be recognized as genocide against them, creating a post-war memory politics which resembled 1980s arguments about World War II [246: 22; 318; 357: 68–9]. The competition over collective victimhood often crowded out acknowledgement of violence committed in the name of one's own nation, reducing the history of the Yugoslav wars to a clash between national narratives [246]. To make visible such dynamics, scholars needed freedom to critically question historical narratives and to examine the politics of knowledge about the past. With this, however, came a responsibility not to cast doubt on evidence that verifiable massacres occurred [45; 47; 315: 110–4].

The end of the 1991–95 wars

A chain of military events after Srebrenica led to the end of the fighting in Bosnia-Herzegovina and Croatia. On 22 July, Izetbegović made a pact with Tuđman to defend Bihać, on the other side of Bosnia, against the VRS [74: 395]. The Croatian Army had strengthened its strategic position against the RSK since January 1992 [151]. In January 1993 it had reconnected Dalmatia and northern Croatia. It then tried to retake the 'Medak pocket' around Gospić in September 1993 (eventually the subject of several war-crimes investigations against Croatian soldiers (Chapter 7)). After the Washington Agreements, the Croatian Army received assistance from a US private military contractor [263: 276]. This stronger force retook Western Slavonia from the RSK in Operation Flash (*Bljesak*) in May 1995. The Tuđman–Izetbegović agreement in late July 1995 meant the Croatian Army could plan another offensive, Operation Storm (*Oluja*). This crossed the Bihać pocket and struck the core of RSK territory [3: 367–76].

The RSK quickly capitulated to the Croatian Army – indeed, one Croatian military historian (against the grain of Croatian post-war public memory) called Oluja much more an RSK loss than a Croatian victory [185: 75–83] – and Croatian forces triumphantly entered Knin on 8 August [99: 296–301]. While approximately 200,000 Serbs fled the Croatian advance, Croatian soldiers and paramilitaries burned Serb houses and killed 500–700 elderly Serbs who remained [29: 464; 381: 84–5]. Oluja was remembered in Croatia as an act of national liberation concluding the Homeland War, and in Serbia as a series of war crimes against Serb civilians: yet another key moment in the Yugoslav wars around which incompatible collective narratives still circulated [344].

After Oluja, the International Contact Group reopened negotiations with Tuđman, Izetbegović and Milošević. All three met at a US airbase at Dayton, Ohio in November 1995 to agree a constitutional and political peace settlement for Bosnia-Herzegovina (the 'Dayton Peace Agreement'). 'Dayton' retained the previous plans' 'ethnic principle'. The post-Dayton Bosnian state contained two units, Republika Srpska and the 'Federation of Bosnia-Herzegovina' (with the status of one strategic town, Brčko, to be determined). The RS, a unitary entity, corresponded to the wartime Republika Srpska. The Federation, corresponding to the ARBiH/HVO alliance, contained its own federal government plus ten self-governing 'cantons', each conceived as Bosniak-majority, Croat-majority or mixed. Vetoes and representation guarantees were intended to stop any one ethnic group being excluded from power, and a (NATO, not UN) foreign military force would oversee the demilitarization and handover of territory.

Time revealed that Dayton placed high expectations on internationally-led 'peacebuilding' as the path to reconstruction and stability, while insufficiently challenging wartime bases of ethno-politics and patronage (Chapter 6). The late 1990s, however, revealed another limitation: the Dayton talks left unaddressed the issue that had arguably catalyzed the 1980s crisis, Albanians' status in Kosovo [282: 10–1]. This weakened the leading Kosovar Albanian political representative, Ibrahim Rugova, and created space for an armed organization, the Kosovo Liberation Army (KLA), to start fighting Serbian security forces. When the Serbian state's campaign against the KLA turned against Albanians' villages in 1998 and NATO demanded Milošević stop the offensive, the ensuing 'Kosovo War' made the south-eastern part of former Yugoslavia the focus of the last phase of the wars.

5 The Kosovo War and Its Aftermath

The Kosovo War (1998–99), the only phase where fighting occurred within Serbia, ended with Kosovo becoming an autonomous UN-administered area and Albanians still campaigning for independence. The war's outcomes also weakened Milošević's position, altered Macedonian politics, and further loosened links between Serbia and Montenegro – background issues in 1991–95 which now entered the foreground of politics. Because of this timing, the first histories of the Yugoslav wars did not integrate Kosovo well: mid-1990s works could allude to Kosovo as a potential future zone of instability and a source of evidence about Milošević's regime, but could not know the outcome, and some so heavily emphasized the Serb/Croat relationship that Kosovo remained sidelined. By 1998, however, the escalation made it possible to represent Kosovo as an imminent Balkan flashpoint – and to more successfully propose books on Kosovo to publishers. In 1998–99, several separate works on Kosovo appeared, giving Anglophone readers more detailed historical background [286; 287; 293]. Like the literature on Bosnia, they evaluated evidence about ethnic coexistence and antagonism on short- and long-term scales. However, their coverage of the internationalization of the Kosovo War was initially only an addendum.

In 1999, 'Kosovo' became an international crisis when NATO used air-strikes against the Federal Republic of Yugoslavia (FRY). After Milošević capitulated, the UN started administering Kosovo, while Milošević fell from power in Serbia the next year. The war also had repercussions in Macedonia, where some Kosovo Liberation Army (KLA) veterans born in Macedonia were involved in a briefer armed conflict in 2001. Debates about its wider regional effects are therefore scattered throughout specialist literature on several post-Yugoslav states: how did it affect Milošević and the opposition in Serbia, relations between Macedonian Slavs and Albanians in the Former Yugoslav Republic of Macedonia, or the balance between Serbia and Montenegro in what still officially remained of Yugoslavia? Today's historians can begin pulling this together. Assessing the Kosovo War, however, should begin with experiences in Kosovo and Serbia under Milošević.

Serbia and Kosovo under Milošević, 1989–98

Scholars of 1990s Serbia have chiefly been interested in the political mobilization of the Serbian public by Milošević and the opposition. Although Serbia's territory was not on the frontline in 1991–95, the conflict still affected the 'Federal Republic of Yugoslavia' (the name given to Serbia and Montenegro after 27 April 1992). UN economic sanctions against FRY caused hyperinflation, shortages and power-cuts for the public, and quick enrichment for criminals who could smuggle goods over borders. Young men faced conscription into the Yugoslav People's Army (JNA) and could expect to be sent to fight. Hundreds of men, and a few women, volunteered for nominally-independent paramilitary units. But of all the countries involved in the Yugoslav wars, Serbia had the largest anti-war protests and the most draft-dodging. Several alternative social organizations founded the 'Centre for Anti-War Action' in July 1991 to co-ordinate protests and support war resisters [145: 491]. Another organization founded in October 1991, Women in Black, campaigned against patriarchal militarism, holding weekly vigils in Belgrade. Campaigners estimated that 50–80 per cent of conscripted men throughout Serbia, and maybe 85 per cent in Belgrade, resisted service [14: 2–3]. The complexities of war participation in Serbia expose the limitations of generalizations about the national character of Serbs or any other people.

Milošević retained power throughout the 1990s (president of Serbia to 1997 then president of FRY until 2000). One explanation has been his control over political, social and economic institutions. The media, as in 1988–91, presented Serbs with Milošević's preferred narrative of national victimhood [21; 29: 497; 35; 142; 146: 422]. Monopolizing the financial system, he nurtured an 'overlapping' economic, political and criminal elite [139: 213]. Several scholars remark on his capacity to inspire public support through references to folkloric symbols and national myths [130; 149]. Another interpretation emphasizes demobilization, or Milošević's capacity to interfere with activities seeking different political or social courses. Repressing independent media was part of this 'destruction of alternatives', but so were the poverty and shortages caused by sanctions, which broke down people's everyday social autonomy [133: 195–8]. Demobilization ensured the existing elite stayed in power and could profit from privatizing the former Yugoslav state's assets [14: 116–19].

Serbia did not have one unified opposition; instead, various movements opposed Milošević for different reasons. Milošević's major early-1990s rivals (and intermittent partners), Vuk Drašković and Vojislav Šešelj, had nationalist, patriarchal programmes and argued Milošević was not protecting Serbs' national interests successfully. Šešelj founded a self-proclaimed new Četnik movement, later renamed the Serbian Radical Party (SRS). Drašković and Šešelj both established paramilitary units ('the 'Serbian Guard' and 'White Eagles') which operated in Croatia and Bosnia-Herzegovina, and Šešelj also instigated persecution of tens of thousands of Croats in Vojvodina [137: 357–9]. The Democratic Party, led by Zoran Đinđić, called for greater democratization within Serbia. Outside parliament was a smaller, explicitly anti-nationalist/anti-militarist opposition connected to Belgrade independent media [132; 145]. In 1996, Drašković, Đinđić and the Civic Alliance of Serbia formed a coalition, 'Zajedno' ('Together'), to contest federal and local elections in November. SPS won the federal elections, but Zajedno won local elections in 14 cities [146: 285]. When Milošević refused to recognize these, Zajedno and student councils co-ordinated three months of demonstrations.

In Kosovo, Milošević's rule was openly authoritarian from the moment he revoked its provincial autonomy in 1989. In summer 1990, Albanian-language broadcasting and the main Albanian newspaper were banned, revoking Albanians' previous cultural rights [293: 217]. Albanian-language schools received a new curriculum to prevent teachers teaching 'subversive' material. Fifteen thousand Albanians lost public-sector jobs, and police dispersed any demonstrations by Albanians [287: 201; 289: 805–6]. Albanian educators and health-workers re-established their workplaces as a poorly-funded 'parallel state' outside official Serbian structures [284; 289]. Politically, Albanians were represented by Ibrahim Rugova's Democratic League of Kosovo (LDK), founded in December 1989. The popularity of Rugova and his non-violent resistance strategy declined after 1995 when Dayton suggested the window for Yugoslav successor states becoming independent was over [293: 287–8]. Meanwhile, a group of Albanians abroad had started funding, arming and recruiting a guerrilla force, the KLA. Its popularity rose as the LDK's declined [285]. The KLA started operating in Kosovo in 1995–96, attacking FRY police stations and gaining control of villages, and announced itself publicly in 1997 [288].

In 1998, the FRY authorities sent troops from the Army of Yugoslavia (VJ, the former JNA) and volunteer paramilitaries to reinforce the soldiers and anti-terrorist police already in Kosovo. Their operation began in the Drenica valley. One KLA commander there, Adem Jashari, became a symbolic national martyr for the KLA when he and his extended family were killed in a shoot-out with Serbian police at Prekaz in March 1998 [277]. By autumn 1998, the Serbian operations had killed several thousand Albanians and forced 230,000 more from their homes [282: 13]. The United Nations Security Council (UNSC) called for a cease-fire. Milošević agreed in October 1998, but resumed operations in December. The massacre of 40 Albanians at Račak on 15 January 1999 prompted NATO to threaten Milošević with air-strikes unless he agreed a peace deal for Kosovo [276: 103–4]. These talks began at Rambouillet on 6 February 1999.

NATO intervention and the fall of Milošević

At Rambouillet, delegations representing the FRY authorities and the Kosovo Albanians were expected to negotiate an agreement on Kosovo's status. The Rambouillet proposals included demobilizing the KLA, stationing a NATO force in Kosovo, and reaching a political settlement for Kosovo within three years. The FRY authorities would not accept the degree of freedom of movement NATO expected from them, nor potential independence for Kosovo. Critics of NATO have suggested Milošević was always supposed to reject Rambouillet, whereas critics of Milošević suggest he opted to reject a genuine proposal in order to continue expelling Albanians from Kosovo [278: 226]. On 18 March, under continued threat of air-strikes, the FRY delegation refused to sign. When Milošević still had not signed by NATO's 24 March deadline, NATO began its air campaign, 'Operation Allied Force'. Controversially, this occurred without UNSC authorization, because Russia and China had threatened to veto any such resolution.

Operation Allied Force aimed to destroy FRY military capacity and prevent it continuing operations in Kosovo. It targeted not only military installations and convoys but also, more controversially, industrial facilities with dual civilian/military uses. Strikes on targets such as the Zastava factory in Kragujevac, the Pančevo oil refinery and municipal power supplies caused significant economic and environmental damage, and 16 Radio–Television Serbia employees were killed in a strike on the broadcaster's headquarters in Belgrade. One strike hit a refugee convoy near Đakovica. The NATO bombing was the first time territory in Serbia or Montenegro had been directly attacked during the 1990s. Protestors casting themselves as defiant underdogs demonstrated against NATO on city squares and bridges [135]. Meanwhile, Milošević shut down independent media, and the opposition journalist Slavko Ćuruvija was murdered in Belgrade. In Kosovo, paramilitaries continued burning and looting Albanian homes. The International Criminal Tribunal for the Former Yugoslavia (ICTY) increased pressure on Milošević by publicly indicting him for Kosovo-related war crimes, the first such indictment for a sitting head of state [363: 38–9].

On 9 June, Milošević agreed UN administration over Kosovo, and NATO's ground force ('KFOR') entered Kosovo from Macedonia. The end of Serbian rule there encouraged Albanian refugees to return, while after KLA reprisals in summer–autumn 1999, tens of thousands of Serbs left Kosovo [280: 286–96]. Serbian forces had killed 10,000–12,000 Albanian civilians, and the United Nations High Commissioner for Refugees (UNHCR) calculated that 848,000 Albanians became refugees [29: 517; 280: 250]. The FRY stated 600 members of its security forces were killed [278: 231–2]. Human Rights Watch attributed another 500 deaths to NATO operations but did not tabulate these by ethnicity [283: 161].

Kosovo was also a key moment in post-Cold War international relations. NATO, the FRY and the KLA could all address a global public directly through the internet, and one scholar termed Kosovo 'the first internet war' [281]. The conflict also exposed tensions among diplomatic principles [294]: when should the national self-determination principle trump existing states' territorial unity? And, the key question concerning foreign intervention, when should the presumption against the use of force be set aside to protect human rights? Liberal interventionists praised the USA, UK and NATO for recognizing early warning-signs of ethnic cleansing and, they argued, acting in time to prevent genocide [268; 279]. Meanwhile, a radical left critique viewed the intervention as a neo-imperialist offensive to forcibly change an inimical sovereign state's regime [19; 261; 275]. The controversy would recur after 9/11 over Afghanistan and Iraq.

Milošević's loss in Kosovo led to his further repression of independent media in Serbia. His rule, however, ended in October 2000 when mass protests against him not recognizing another election result forced him to resign. The protests concerned the September 2000 FRY presidential elections, where the main opposition candidate Vojislav Koštunica had stood against Milošević. The official result did recognize Koštunica had won but quoted a figure that would have required another run-off election. The opposition stated Koštunica should already have won outright, and called demonstrations and a general strike. The student group Otpor, which had been organizing non-violent resistance since 1996–97, encouraged young people to participate with eye-catching campaigns [316: 63], circulating parody images of Milošević and branding their posters with a raised-fist protest logo and the slogan 'Gotov je!' ('He's finished!'). Miners at Kolubara joined the strike on 29 September, and their protest's escalation was arguably the 'turning point' in overthrowing Milošević [140: 24–5; 147: 3–9]. On 5 October, protestors from elsewhere in Serbia travelled to Belgrade to join the demonstrations, which stormed the Serbian parliament building [127]. The army and police refused to repress the protests as Milošević ordered, and Milošević resigned. On 1 April 2001, his former 'myth of [...] invincibility' was punctured when he was arrested for extradition to the ICTY [315: 31].

'5 October' appeared a victory for peaceful protest, but also had a less visible dimension: Đinđić, one of the coalition leaders, had obtained the agreement of a special forces commander, the gangster Milorad Ulemek-Legija, not to fire on any protesters [127: 27–9]. Milošević's downfall was not as simple as a popular uprising against his repression, or indeed as an angry outburst about his losing control over Kosovo. However, Milošević's authoritarian actions during and after the Kosovo War, plus the economic damage the air-strikes caused, weakened his ability to demobilize the opposition in 2000 compared to before 1999. His former allies in business and the security services then began to withdraw their support [142: 26].

Macedonia and the 'Albanian question'

The Kosovo War made the so-called 'Albanian question' more prominent in discourses about peace and security in south-east Europe. It had particular consequences in Macedonia, where Albanians were a minority (officially 22.9 per cent of the 1.95 million population in 1994) and the 'constituent people' of the Yugoslav republic were Macedonian South Slavs (66.5 per cent of the population in 1994) [29: 574]. Nationalism had gradually replaced Communism as the dominant principle in Macedonian politics after Yugoslavia collapsed. Macedonia's first multi-party elections (November 1990) returned a well-known Party official, Kiro Gligorov, as president and non-Communist nationalists, VMRO–DPMNE, as the largest parliamentary party. While Gligorov joined Izetbegović in the pan-Yugoslav confederal proposal, VMRO–DPMNE pushed for independence. A Macedonian independence referendum on 8 September 1991 was successful. However, most Albanians boycotted it, with grievances including the closure of Albanian-language schools and, they argued, Albanians being deliberately undercounted in the April 1991 census [301: 21]. Macedonia's new constitution in November 1991 defined Macedonia as the national state of the Macedonian people.

Tito's Yugoslavia had been the first regime to acknowledge – some would even say create – a Macedonian language and history distinguishing Macedonians from Bulgarians and Serbs.

Macedonian national sovereignty was easier to imagine in 1992 than 1945. The strengthening of a Macedonian national identity had, however, worsened Yugoslavia's relations with Greece in the 1980s, since Greek foreign policy rejected the idea of Macedonians as a nation [302: 167–9]. The Greek state also rejected 'Macedonia' for the name of a sovereign country, and international recognition was delayed until April 1993 under a compromise name, 'the Former Yugoslav Republic of Macedonia' (FYROM). This dispute ultimately concerned which national group had the right to claim ancient Macedonia and its past [298: 154]. Within Macedonia, the nation/state link was contested differently: Albanians called for Macedonia to be a genuinely bi-national state, not one where Albanians were only a minority.

During the Kosovo War, hundreds of thousands of Albanian and Roma refugees from Kosovo fled to hastily-established refugee camps in Macedonia and Albania. Many returned, but the KLA's operations had meanwhile created cross-border transit networks that paramilitaries and organized criminals would continue to use. A small group called the 'Liberation Army of Preševo, Medveđa and Bujanovac', using left-over weapons, had launched attacks on police in southern Serbia in 1999–2000, using some northern Macedonian villages for support [295: 128–9]. A more serious insurgency occurred in Macedonia in 2001. Two KLA co-founders, Ali Ahmeti and Fazli Veliu, who had been born in Macedonia, used their recruitment and smuggling networks to form a 'National Liberation Army' (NLA) there [288: 234–7].

The NLA was smaller and more elite than the KLA but used the same tactics of attacking police stations and taking control of villages. In February 2001, it launched an attack in the Tetovo area which lasted until August. The Macedonian government fought back, and the interior minister, Ljube Boškoski, started forming a paramilitary unit ('the Lions') to attack NLA-controlled villages. More than 100 people were killed before an agreement was signed in Ohrid on 13 August 2001, promising Albanians greater rights in exchange for the NLA's disarmament. The Ohrid Agreement moved away from the idea that Macedonian South Slavs owned the state, though some degree of Macedonian/Albanian separation in education and media persisted [303].

Less has been written on the NLA insurgency than other post-Yugoslav conflicts, and pre-2001 works could have not have covered it. It has been explained with reference to the 'import' of violence from Kosovo, to an expansionist position in Albanian nationalism, and to Macedonian state policy towards Albanians [297]. While it did not become a protracted war, it attracted similar questions to those about the others. Should the explanatory emphasis be on ethnic division [300: 134], or less on presupposing division and more on perceiving how ethnic boundaries were actually created by people's everyday practices [301]? Were ethnicized conflicts like the 2001 insurgency better explained with reference to long-term nationalist expansion programmes or short-term social and criminal circumstances [295]? And how did other aspects of identity and power after socialism intersect with ethnic identification [299]? For all these reasons, Macedonia deserves a place in the history of the Yugoslav wars.

The end of the Federal Republic of Yugoslavia

The mid-2000s also saw the final fragmentation of the Serbia–Montenegro union that succeeded socialist Yugoslavia. The FRY was a two-republic federation between April 1992 and February 2003, when the FRY parliament reconstituted it as a looser 'state union' officially called 'Serbia and Montenegro'. 'Yugoslavia' then stopped denoting any existing state, although the Yugoslav idea in the sense of unifying all South Slavs into one state had ceased to exist by at the very latest June 1991. Between 1992 and 2003, Montenegro's relations with the Milošević-dominated FRY institutions showed that even the political unification of Serbs and Montenegrins was in question: by 1996, the Montenegrin Prime Minister, Milo Đukanović, was already criticizing Milošević and trying to attract foreign investment independently. Đukanović won Montenegro's presidential elections in July 1997 and by 2000 had made Montenegro a 'separate economic space', changing its currency to the Deutschmark and then the euro [94: 449–59].

'5 October' increased expectations for reform and democratization. In December 2000, the Democratic Party leader Zoran Đinđić was elected prime minister of Serbia, while Koštunica was FRY president. Đinđić, unlike Koštunica, believed Serbia should reform rapidly and prepare for European integration, including co-operation with the ICTY. He was instrumental in achieving

Milošević's extradition. Đinđić raised hopes among the urban middle class disenfranchized by Milošević, but was unpopular among those whose vested interests were threatened by his crackdown on corruption [316]. He was shot dead on 12 March 2003. Amid public mourning, the government declared a state of emergency and arrested dozens of people with criminal connections, including the 'Zemun Clan' network around Legija. Legija and an associate who had shot Đinđić were convicted of murder in 2007. However, many of Milošević's patronage networks stayed intact, while the opposition coalition fell apart.

Post-Đinđić Serbia struggled with corruption and a ruined economy that worsened after the 2008 global financial crisis [147: 63–7; 316]. Parliamentary politics, however, revolved around other concerns: politicians such as Koštunica (prime minister in 2004–8) and SRS's Tomislav Nikolić (president of Serbia since 2012) continued to set agendas around nationalism, whereas the 2004–12 president, Boris Tadić, openly aligned himself with a 'European Serbia'. A symbol of this division became the state's failure to protect Pride marches from far-right violence. The government supported Pride in 2010 and 2014, but cancelled other parades rather than confront far-right groups and the Church [335; 338].

Meanwhile, Đukanović continued extricating Montenegro from FRY, and called an independence referendum for 21 May 2006. The vote for independence was close (55.5 per cent to 45.5 per cent), but still met the EU's recognition criteria [88: 218]. Montenegro declared independence on 3 June 2006 and the Serbia–Montenegro union, the last remnant of Yugoslavia, ended. The close result reflected two narratives of Montenegrin identity that had competed throughout the twentieth century [88]: were Montenegrins a specific subset of Serbs, shaped by a history of living in the mountains and rebelling against Ottoman rule, or had that very history made Montenegrin culture distinct enough to belong to a separate nation that should govern itself? The Montenegrin question was not resolved through war, and so histories of the wars covered Montenegro minimally, though it still belonged within the wider history of the break-up of Yugoslavia.

The FRY's formal dissolution did not include resolving the status of Kosovo, which was still under UN administration. A new Albanian political elite had formed around the ex-KLA.

The United Nations Mission in Kosovo (UNMIK) and other international agencies were supposed to oversee the creation of liberal democratic institutions, though critics called them an unaccountable international 'protectorate' [350]. Few Serbs trusted UNMIK or KFOR. In December 1999, a 'Serb National Council' in Mitrovica was founded to co-ordinate self-government in the four northern municipalities with large Serb majorities. Mitrovica experienced Albanian-led riots in 2004 and Serb-led riots in 2008, both focusing on a bridge between Serb-majority and Albanian-majority districts. Internationally, the USA and UK attempted to negotiate an independence pathway for Kosovo, and the UN negotiator Martti Ahtisaari also recommended independence in March 2007 [282: 64]. The Serbian government, supported by Russia, refused to give up sovereignty over Kosovo. Amid this deadlock, the Kosovo parliament unilaterally declared independence on 17 February 2008. Kosovo would be recognized by more than 100 countries, including the USA, UK and Germany, but not for instance Russia, China, Greece or Spain.

By the mid-2010s, Kosovo, Serbia, Montenegro and Macedonia all had separate political trajectories. The Kosovo War had nonetheless altered all their politics. Perhaps most momentously for the region, it weakened Milošević's standing with elite allies and contributed to his fall in 2000. That fall could easily be narrated as a natural end-point for the Yugoslav wars, but studying the post-Milošević period helped historians assess the conflicts' longer-term consequences. Insights from studying peacebuilding and reconciliation, war crimes trials, or post-conflict languages and cultures illuminated the consequences of the destruction of multi-ethnic communities and the appropriation of Yugoslav state resources during the Yugoslav wars, in turn opening new directions for historians of the 1990s.

6 Peacebuilding, Reconciliation and Reconstruction

The conflicts in Croatia, Bosnia-Herzegovina, Kosovo and Macedonia all ended with peace settlements that aimed to state how ethnic groups and their political representatives would coexist within each country. The war in Slovenia, too, had ended after negotiations (the July 1991 Brioni Declaration), though without such detailed provisions about Slovenia's internal ethno-political affairs. The post-1995 peace settlements had several things in common. They implied that guarantees about ethnic minorities' status were necessary to prevent future wars. Moreover, they continued the link between ethno-national identity and territorial sovereignty that had underpinned twentieth-century state-building in south-east Europe. They also incorporated international supervision and monitoring, and so international bodies such as the UN and EU, foreign governments with interests in south-east Europe, and non-governmental organizations influenced post-Yugoslav domestic politics. In Bosnia-Herzegovina and Kosovo, international agencies were even part of the post-war political structure.

International organizations' intended role was not just deterring further hostilities, but also promoting values which their members believed would create lasting peace: democratization, the free market, and the rule of law. Former Yugoslavia thus became a major site of the post-Cold War approach to international intervention known as 'peacebuilding'. Peacebuilding, unlike peacekeeping, took place after, not during, conflicts; it involved politically and economically reshaping countries so that their causes of conflict would become things of the past. The questions asked about post-Yugoslav peacebuilding are helpful for reflecting on the dynamics and consequences of the 1990s wars. Some, again, are about inter-ethnic relations: since ethnic separation had been an aim and consequence of the wars, how far did the peace settlements alter it? Others are about the power relations of peacebuilding: if international agencies and their values were so central to peacebuilding, did this end up restraining local people's political capacity or even post-Yugoslav states' sovereignty? The weightiest question is perhaps whether the intended outcomes of peacebuilding achieved meaningful reconciliation between people and stable reconstruction of their societies.

Debating the Bosnian settlement

The first peacebuilding initiative to be assessed was 'Dayton', which ended the Bosnian war and heavily involved the UN and NATO in post-conflict Bosnia-Herzegovina. In fact there had also been post-conflict UN activity in Croatia, but on a much smaller scale: eastern Slavonia had been under transitional UN administration ('UNTAES') in preparation for reintegration into Croatia, and when UNTAES withdrew in January 1998, Tuđman could declare Croatia's sovereignty complete. Until 2002, UN observers ('UNMOP') in the Prevlaka peninsula also supervised demilitarization at the Croatian–Montenegrin border. There is very little scholarly debate about the Croatia missions, and indeed eastern Slavonia and Prevlaka have themselves been under-researched in comparison to Krajina. There is much more on the consequences of Dayton, which configured a new Bosnian state structure and involved international agencies in administering the whole country.

Scholarly disciplines initially asked disparate questions about peacebuilding in post-conflict Bosnia. Political and legal analyses concentrated on institutional and electoral politics [307]. Anthropologists, meanwhile, found these studies' information valuable but their perspectives incomplete. The *New Bosnian Mosaic* volume collected anthropological studies based on fieldwork in Bosnian communities to demonstrate the value of '[a]n approach "from below"' [308: 27]. The editors argued this made it possible to move beyond the interpretive framework of wartime scholarship, which had concentrated on whether to call the conflict aggression or civil war, antagonism/coexistence in long-term inter-ethnic history, and debating foreign intervention. They identified ethno-politics, collective memories and the international agencies as the main themes in research on post-war Bosnia, but suggested 'local-level realities defy reduction to such simple categories' [308: 19]. Political scientists went on to use ethnography to examine how state power or multinational reconciliation initiatives manifested themselves locally [329; 358; 372]. Studies on Bosnia, and Kosovo, thus contributed to a broader 'local turn' in peacebuilding research.

Establishing the Federation and Republika Srpska as constitutional entities within Bosnia-Herzegovina required territorial and prisoner exchanges in early 1996. NATO's multinational military force (IFOR, the 'Implementation Force') monitored this and enforced Dayton's arms reduction provisions. Handover was nonetheless an insecure time for many Bosnians. In February–March 1996, when VRS-occupied suburbs of Sarajevo were being transferred to Federation control, the retreating VRS authorities burned out apartment buildings and convinced approximately 60,000 Serbs to leave [215: 97–9; 219: 360; 222: 338–40]. In April, groups of Bosniak refugees trying to return to homes that were now in the Republika Srpska (RS) demonstrated against RS authorities and IFOR troops who were preventing them going back [252: 167–72].

Elections for the Bosnia-wide House of Representatives and collective presidency were held quickly – some said too early – in September 1996 [29: 471–7]. The Party of Democratic Action (SDA), the Croatian Democratic Union (HDZ) and the Serb Democratic Party (SDS) – the three major nationalist parties – won both. Except in 2000–2, when the multi-ethnic Social Democratic Party (SDP) had a parliamentary majority, nationalist coalitions dominated post-war Bosnian politics. In the Federation, SDA remained strong, as (despite occasional splits) did HDZ. In RS, SDS predominated until 2006, with its so-called 'Banja Luka' faction prevailing over Karadžić's closest associates (the 'Pale' faction) in 1998. In 2006, however, Milorad Dodik and his Alliance of Independent Social Democrats (SNSD) won the RS parliamentary elections. Dodik's late-1990s reputation had been moderate, but in the mid-2000s he started supporting the idea of an RS independence referendum – raising, for his critics, alarming parallels with the November 1991 SDS referendum [348: 170]. With politics dominated by nationalism, multi-ethnic parties such as SDP or Naša Stranka ('Our Party'), formed by several civil-society groups in 2008, not only had to propose more attractive policies but also to challenge the very bases of nationalist patronage in order to win [349]. Their problem was similar to that of non-nationalist political alternatives in 1989–90 except that nationalism was structured even further into politics. By 2014, when the 'plenum' protests against corruption, privatization and nationalism took place [304], non-nationalist positions remained marginalized in the formal political sphere.

Objections to Dayton had various grounds. Some accepted its principles but argued that it should have divided territory differently: for instance, the Bosnian HDZ often argued there should have been a separate 'Bosnian Croat' entity [252: 283]. Other critiques went further than just rejecting Dayton's actual provisions; they also rejected its underlying link between ethnicity and territory [252; 258]. David Campbell's provocative term 'apartheid cartography' implied Dayton had created ethnically-separated spaces (the cantons, and the Federation/RS division) despite official rhetoric about Bosnia-Herzegovina being multi-ethnic [252]. Similarly, the post-war Bosnian constitution (an annex to Dayton) was criticized for grounding Bosnians' political representation in membership of one of three constituent peoples (Bosniaks, Croats and Serbs). Bosnia's collective presidency had to have one Bosniak, one Serb and one Croat representative, yet that ruled out potential candidates who identified themselves differently. In 2009, two Roma and Jewish representatives, Dervo Sejdić and Jakob Finci, successfully challenged this at the European Court of Human Rights, which ruled Bosnia-Herzegovina would have to alter its constitution. Meanwhile, expressions of ethnic identity beyond Bosniak, Serb or Croat became invisible in Bosnian demographic data, and schools followed separate Bosniak, Croat or Serb programmes of study – sometimes even when students were in the same building [321; 334: 79–80; 414: 192–3]. Anti-essentialists considered these constitutional, territorial and political practices impeded solidarity across ethnic boundaries and thus interfered with a genuine democratic pluralism that would have built a stronger peace [336].

The international politics of peacebuilding

Post-conflict peacebuilding, like wartime foreign intervention, reflected broader developments in post-Cold-War international relations. In 1989–91, the collapse of Communism and the USSR suggested to many Western policymakers that political and economic liberalism had been proven the best possible political system and could now spread worldwide. This provided another rationale for extending international oversight into the post-conflict building of liberal democratic institutions, and there had been several shorter-term initiatives before 1995 (for instance in Cambodia, Angola and Rwanda). Whereas UNTAES was also short-term, Bosnia-Herzegovina and Kosovo were much longer-term international commitments, and after 1999 this more extensive model became an established pattern in post-conflict governance (for instance in East Timor, Sierra Leone and Liberia).

'International administration' involved international agencies in domestic politics as well as humanitarian relief and security [309]. Dayton, for instance, created an 'Office of the High Representative' (OHR), overseeing civilian and political affairs. Seven European diplomats, all male, had served as High Representative to date. In 1997 the High Representative gained the 'Bonn Powers' to pass laws if elected representatives could not agree and to remove elected officials whom he considered were obstructing Dayton. UNMIK's remit, in Kosovo, extended beyond political oversight into civil administration, though Kosovo authorities took over most administrative functions after 2008. Both countries provided important examples for International Relations debates about peacebuilding and the so-called 'liberal peace', the theory that building democratic institutions in post-conflict states would prevent future war.

David Chandler's early-2000s critique of peacebuilding argued international institutions experimentally redefined their post-Cold War organizational, political and strategic relationships in Bosnia-Herzegovina and that BiH/Kosovo became precedents for Western post-conflict democratization in Iraq and Afghanistan [310; 311]. Others followed him in criticizing the BiH/Kosovo international administrations for denying local people autonomy while stating they were empowering them and for only being accountable abroad [323; 350]. One rejoinder to these critiques was to argue that, though some liberal peacebuilding practices were flawed, the principles were still better than no international response [340]. Another response was recognizing 'post-liberal' or 'hybrid' forms of peace that emerged from local, everyday engagement with – or resistance to – liberal peacebuilding [332]. In Bosnia-Herzegovina, these included cultural centres, community groups, small religious organizations and ad-hoc social movements, none of which easily fitted into international agencies' working practices [330].

A historical dimension to critiquing liberal peacebuilding related it to older forms of international governance and global structural inequalities. Some compared peacebuilding closely with colonialism [101; 323], and one study even likened the OHR's administrative powers to British rule in India by calling it 'a European Raj' [331: 70]. Liberals, however, argued peacebuilding/imperialism comparisons were mistaken because peacebuilding had not sought to extract wealth from colonized territory [340: 348–50]. The problem of structural power imbalances in peacebuilding could be addressed theoretically or through fieldwork-based research into the everyday practices of international staff [319] – approaching anthropologists' micro-local lens. Localized studies also proved invaluable in assessing reconciliation and reconstruction outside institutional peacebuilding.

Reconciliation and reconstruction beyond peacebuilding

The goals of peacebuilding could be described as 'reconciliation' and 'reconstruction' – rebuilding states and societies so that conflict could not reoccur [314]. What however might reconciliation be, and how far was it achieved or even possible after ethnopolitical violence and genocide? Some anthropologists suggested there could be reconciliation as day-to-day peaceful coexistence without relationships and trust necessarily regenerating fully, and 'functional' or 'thin' reconciliation might be more feasible than transformative or 'thick' reconciliation given the state of postwar politics [317]. They also noted that discussing reconciliation always included assumptions about which sides were being reconciled. The dominant international concept of reconciliation in former Yugoslavia, it appeared, was about reconciliation between ethnic nations [314]. Yet if the wars were seen only as a conflict between ethnic groups, equally important dimensions such as

94

organized crime, or competition for economic resources among party-political elites, were overlooked [325]. This returned to one of the overarching problems in interpreting the wars – how far they should be considered wars 'about' ethnicity. Anthropological assessments of post-conflict peacebuilding thus reiterated this question's importance for understanding the 1990s.

Any reconciliation and reconstruction, however, faced the obstacle that much of what had been destroyed could not be rebuilt. Although demographers were still verifying precise death-tolls more than a decade later, adding most recent figures for each conflict gave an approximate total of 140,000. In Bosnia-Herzegovina, a 2007 study by the Research and Documentation Centre (RDC) found 97,207 people had been directly killed by military violence and 39,684 had been civilians (83 per cent of the civilians were Bosniaks, 10 per cent Serbs, and 5 per cent Croats). This matched ICTY calculations from 2005, but was controversial among Bosnians because the wartime Sarajevo government had stated figures of 200,000–250,000 [245; 251]. In 2009, the Croatian human rights organization Documentation began a similar project to confirm deaths on both sides in Croatia; their analysts cited previous estimates that 14,000–16,000 non-Serbs and 6,222 Serbs had died [368: 86]. Marko Attila Hoare, reviewing overall death-tolls, noted there had been more detailed demographic analyses for Bosnia-Herzegovina than Croatia or Kosovo. He cited figures of between 10,356–12,000 Albanian deaths during the Kosovo War, though available data could not clarify how many Albanians had been non-combatants or how many Serbs had died [368: 86]. Across the region, tens of thousands more fates remained unknown. The International Commission for Missing Persons reported that 40,000 people were originally reported missing after the Yugoslav wars, 30,000 from Bosnia-Herzegovina; by 2012, according to an ICMP report, 14,000 were still unaccounted-for. Their uncertain fate left families unable to grieve and contributed to mistrust within communities.

Even survivors could often not resume ordinary life in their former homes. Besides outright obstruction to post-war return in parts of Croatia, Bosnia-Herzegovina and Kosovo, authorities that had been complicit in wartime violence could tacitly make returnees unwelcome. New signs, monuments and graffiti helped to transform towns such as Zvornik or Srebrenica into monoethnic spaces which could themselves intimidate survivors from returning [252: 267–8; 313: 133; 337; 380]. The human environment of home – people's neighbours – had also changed [326]. Frequently, refugees' old homes had either been destroyed or handed to local authorities' supporters (themselves sometimes refugees from elsewhere). Peacebuilding agencies, therefore, had to enforce property restitution schemes: 220,000 refugees made restitution claims in Bosnia-Herzegovina, though only 29,000 did so in Kosovo [351: 298–9]. Often, however, a household would sell its house and then buy another elsewhere, so the demographic effects of ethno-political violence stayed unchanged [346].

Post-war commemorations were also contentious. Across the region, survivors of persecution and atrocities demanded their narratives of the recent past should be recognized in the places where their attackers committed the crimes, through permanent memorials and the right to hold commemorations at memorial sites [313; 333; 337]. Yet in Bosnia-Herzegovina, many sites of atrocities against Bosniaks – including Prijedor, Foča and Srebrenica – were assigned to Republika Srpska at Dayton. Local authorities could interfere with commemorations of VRS atrocities while promoting their own, opposite narrative of 1992–95, which presented the VRS as fighting a defensive war to protect Serbs against ARBiH/HVO aggression [228; 313]. Indeed, in 2007 hundreds of Srebrenica survivors even campaigned for Srebrenica to receive special autonomous status outside RS authority [337]. Banning, vandalizing or removing memorials could be said to erase victims' and survivors' past all over again. However, there were also arguments that (some) commemoration could obstruct reconciliation. One critical reading of the competing Croat and Serb memorials in Vukovar, for instance, suggested that in privileging national victimhood above all else they silenced narratives that did not fit that framework, such as the histories of Serbs who saved Croats or even fought for the Croatian Army [358].

Although most literature on reconciliation viewed it as an inter-ethnic question, the wars affected many other social categories: 'urbanity and rurality, gender, generation, class and occupation', to quote *The New Bosnian Mosaic* [308: 2]. However, the collapse of Yugoslav state socialism is still rarely discussed in as much detail as the wars' ethnic and national dimensions. Scholars need to apply a double lens: the Yugoslav successor states were simultaneously post-conflict *and* post-socialist [305; 306: 861; 318: 39; 326: 186–90]. Property restitution in Bosnia, Croatia or Kosovo, for instance, was complex not just because of forced migration patterns but also because of how much housing the Party used to own. Post-Yugoslav elites took this property over, distributed it clientelistically, and privatized formerly 'socially-owned' factories in equally clientelistic ways [306; 341: 470–1; 351: 299]. People's experiences under Yugoslav socialism left them remembering healthcare, education, social security and employment as entitlements they had had before the war which were now lost [326: 191]. Though socialist rule in Yugoslavia had failed, this legacy contributed to widespread public disillusionment in the post-war successor states.

By the late 2000s, post-Yugoslav political elites had shown they could advance their states' institutional progress towards Euro-Atlantic integration. They had demonstrated much less capacity to meet public demands for jobs, pensions and meaningful mass political participation, to govern without corruption (as trials of two former Slovenian and Croatian prime ministers, Janez Janša and Ivo Sanader, showed in 2012–14), or to sustainably manage the environment. Official peacebuilding had not prioritized socio-economic wellbeing either [342]. After the 2008 global financial crisis, post-Yugoslav activist movements articulated similar critiques during protests against, for instance, redevelopments of public spaces in Zagreb or Banja Luka, the bailout of a Slovenian bank, and an RS/Federation political standoff in Bosnia-Herzegovina that temporarily prevented registration of births [320]. The most sustained popular mobilization against political elites and their practices occurred in spring 2014 when Bosnian citizens' groups ('plenums') demanded cantonal, municipal and federal authorities end corruption and investigate controversial privatizations [304]. These movements were strong signs that public mobilization around something other than ethno-political entitlement could be achieved; the problem was translating this into change in the mainstream political system, where the wartime elites' successors still framed debate. This disconnection between political elites and the public similarly dogged the projects of putting war crimes on trial and creating new public understandings of the wartime past.

7 The Past on Trial

Tribunals both judged the Yugoslav wars and narrated them. The International Criminal Tribunal for the Former Yugoslavia (ICTY), established in 1993, was an integral part of the UN's response to the Bosnian conflict. Its rationale was not only deterrence but also the idea of 'transitional justice': the suggestion that investigating and trying war crimes revealed authoritative evidence and forced post-war societies to 'come to terms with the past'. 'Transitional justice' implied that, for a society to move past wartime antagonisms and find peace, public accountability for the crimes that were committed during a conflict was required. This might occur during war crimes trials or at a 'truth and reconciliation commission' (TRC), which hears testimony but does not pass sentence. Transitional justice was intended as transformative, stabilizing a society's social and political relations, and international institutions were heavily involved; indeed, some argued that making the 'transition' into a new social understanding of history became an international standard for how societies should deal with past crimes after the Yugoslav wars [381: 5]. In the post-conflict intervention model that emerged after the Yugoslav wars, transitional justice, peacebuilding and reconciliation all went together. ICTY activities would have political consequences in several Yugoslav successor states, but not necessarily the consequences that 'transitional justice' theories foresaw.

The post-Yugoslav states, especially Bosnia-Herzegovina and Serbia, became important case-studies for transitional justice scholars who debated what forms of public witnessing were most effective and what the obstacles to transitional justice might be. Historians of other topics too had to take account of the ICTY: its decisions became political issues in post-war Bosnia-Herzegovina, Croatia, Serbia and Kosovo; its trials debated historical narratives;

and it influenced the production of published historical works. Much has been written about the ICTY itself [352; 360; 361; 362; 364; 371; 377; 387; 388]. However, the broader question of how far societies could, or even needed to, 'come to terms with the past' after conflicts like the Yugoslav wars also required a focus on local responses to the problem of interrogating the past.

The establishment of the ICTY

The United Nations Security Council (UNSC) established an international war crimes tribunal for the former Yugoslavia after its Commission of Experts, appointed in October 1992, delivered an interim report on 9 February 1993. The commission was advising the UN on whether evidence of human rights violations in former Yugoslavia suggested breaches of the Geneva Conventions or international humanitarian law. Establishing a tribunal has been interpreted both as a response to 'public outrage' in many UN member states about the images from Bosnia in 1992 [352: 358], and as a means to avoid the pressure for military intervention [385: 34]. In either case, a tribunal was not completely a UN innovation: in May 1991, a journalist from Croatia, Mirko Klarin, had already called for an international 'Nuremberg'-style tribunal to deter the planning of war in Yugoslavia, and in April 1991 the Luxembourg and German foreign ministers had already suggested an international tribunal should investigate Saddam Hussein's persecution of Kurds [364: 33; 377: 12]. The Security Council authorized the tribunal on 25 May 1993, stating it 'would contribute to the restoration and maintenance of peace' [377: 8], and the commission made its final report on 27 May 1994. Its examples included Prijedor, Sarajevo, Dubrovnik and the Medak pocket.

The ICTY both investigated crimes, through the Office of the Prosecutor (OTP), and held trials; its staff included investigators, interpreters/translators, prosecution lawyers and judges. Like the International Court of Justice (ICJ) (the UN's other international court, which had adjudicated lawsuits between states since 1946), the ICTY sat in The Hague. Its statute gave it jurisdiction over all 'grave breaches' of the Geneva Conventions, 'violations of the laws or customs of war', genocide, and crimes against humanity committed on the territory of former Yugoslavia since 1 January

1991 [377: 133–51]. Initially it dealt with Croatia and Bosnia-Herzegovina, but in 1999 it started covering Kosovo, and it also heard a few cases from the 2001 Macedonian conflict. Crimes against humanity included, if committed against civilians during conflict: murder; extermination; enslavement; deportation; imprisonment; torture; rape (not previously named as a crime against humanity in international criminal justice); political, racial and religious persecution; and 'other inhumane acts'. The tribunal existed to try individuals, not organizations or states. However, this still forced it to 'tell an individual story about collective violence' and determine the guilt of specific persons within complex, often deliberately-obscured, organizational structures [385: 39]. At first, it also had to determine that the international laws of war actually applied to its cases: the 'grave breaches of the Geneva Conventions' charges would not have applied if the Yugoslav wars were ruled a civil war within one state, but by 1999–2000 ICTY judges were rejecting this defence [377: 245–6].

In August 1994 the ICTY appointed a Chief Prosecutor, Richard Goldstone, formerly president of the 1991–94 public inquiry into human rights violations in apartheid-era South Africa. Goldstone indicted lower-level figures first to build cases against commanders and leaders later [364: 72]. The ICTY's first indictee, in November 1994, was Dragan Nikolić, commander of a transit camp near Vlasenica in eastern Bosnia where non-Serbs had been imprisoned and tortured. Its first international arrest warrant, also against Nikolić, came in October 1995. Nikolić himself was not arrested until 2000, so the ICTY's first trial was of Duško Tadić. Tadić had been a Serb Democratic Party (SDS) leader from Kozarac, near Prijedor, and was accused of killing and torturing prisoners in the nearby concentration camps as well as participating in the SDS/Army of Republika Srpska (VRS) attack on Kozarac. The ICTY took his case over from Germany, where he had been arrested, and his trial opened in May 1996 [377: 124]. The tribunal convicted Tadić on 11 of 31 charges, rejecting his defence that he had not been living in Prijedor. It sentenced him in May 1997. In the meantime, it had also tried Dražen Erdemović for participating in the Srebrenica massacre. Erdemović, a Croat who had been conscripted into the VRS, handed himself to the ICTY in March 1996 and pleaded guilty [360]. He was sentenced in November 1996.

Prosecutors hoped Erdemović's evidence could help them indict more senior figures, at a time when the ICTY was already under pressure to aim higher. Campaigners had already presented a case for indicting Slobodan Milošević in 1996 [217]. The ICTY did not indict him until 27 May 1999, and initially only over 1998–99 and Kosovo; Milošević's Croatia and Bosnia-Herzegovina indictments followed in November 2001. In the meantime, the ICTY had developed a legal theory of 'joint criminal enterprise' (JCE) for indicting politicians and military commanders. JCE required prosecutors to show that defendants had knowingly shared a criminal purpose, making them collectively responsible for acts committed as part of this plan. This became grounds for prosecuting Milošević and other high-ranking figures, and made prosecutors responsible for proving narratives about the entire wars [165; 385: 37].

Significant trials

In 2015, four ICTY trials were still underway – Goran Hadžić, Radovan Karadžić, Ratko Mladić and Vojislav Šešelj – and 16 more were being appealed. Among the 141 resolved indictments, 18 people had been acquitted, 74 sentenced, 13 had had cases referred to national courts, 20 had had indictments withdrawn and the other 16 had died before or after extradition: one of these was Milošević, whose death in March 2006 curtailed his trial. Slightly more than two-thirds of the total indictees were Serbs [385: 45]. Although space precludes reviewing every case, certain significant judgements and trials shaped the history of transitional justice in the region. There was particular scrutiny of the ICTY's record in prosecuting and convicting defendants on genocide charges, since scholars who called for greater recognition of Republika Srpska's wartime activities as genocidal considered the ICTY weak and ineffective in genocide prosecutions [206: 109–10; 367]. For many years Radislav Krstić, the VRS Drina Corps's deputy commander during the attack on Srebrenica, represented the only genocide-related conviction, yet his April 2004 conviction was for aiding and abetting genocide, not directly perpetrating it. Vujadin Popović and Ljubiša Beara, VRS officers who helped plan the attack, were convicted of genocide in June 2010 [357: 75]. The Krstić judgement suggested direct responsibility would also fall on Mladić, but in 2015 it was still unknown whether the genocide charges against Mladić would succeed. Karadžić had meanwhile been acquitted in 2012 of genocide charges relating to 1992, though his trial on other counts, including genocide at Srebrenica in 1995, continued [363: 31].

The ICTY punished war rape more forthrightly. The 2000–1 trial of three guards from Foča was the first to be solely about rape as a crime against humanity and was thus particularly significant for feminist studies of international criminal justice [355]. So, for another reason, was the trial of Biljana Plavšić, the only woman the ICTY indicted. Plavšić had served on the RS collective presidency throughout the war in Bosnia-Herzegovina and had been RS president in 1996–98. In October 2002 she pleaded guilty to persecution of non-Serbs in Bosnia-Herzegovina between July 1991 and December 1992, controversially having her sentence reduced in exchange for publicly accepting her responsibility.

Several command responsibility cases, meanwhile, ended in acquittals at first hearing. Among these were Sefer Halilović, indicted as the superior officer of Army of the Republic of Bosnia-Herzegovina (ARBiH) troops who killed 13 Croat civilians in September 1993, Milan Milutinović (president of Serbia during the Kosovo War), and Ljube Boškoski (Macedonian interior minister in 2001). This showed that indictments were part of a serious judicial process rather than simply a formality before a guilty verdict. However, the ICTY's capacity to acquit, and to reverse some decisions on appeal, did not protect it from widespread perceptions of bias in the post-Yugoslav states. It was commonly seen as a political court, and inferences about its views on certain nations' collective guilt were regularly drawn from whom it chose or did not choose to indict [17: 178–9; 207; 352; 371]. These controversies shared an expectation that the tribunal should have made meaningful contributions to scholarly and public understanding of the Yugoslav wars.

The sheer amount of evidence the ICTY collected raised expectations that it could interpret the wars as a whole. It might, however, have been misguided to expect a court, with its remit of assessing individual guilt on specific charges, to fulfil this narrative role [382: 177–9]. Other factors too made the ICTY an unstable narrator. It reversed some verdicts on appeal, and never gave some other verdicts because indictees died – sometimes, as with Arkan or the Croatian Army chief of staff Janko Bobetko, before having even been arrested. Milošević's death in custody meant no narrative with the authority of a judgement emerged from the ICTY's most complex case, though evidence released during his trial became useful for scholars [373]. Verdicts reversed on appeal, however, were an even greater challenge to the narrative function projected onto the ICTY, because they made the tribunal appear to reverse a narrative it had already proclaimed.

Several major figures had verdicts reversed on appeal. In 2008, for instance, the ICTY reversed its earlier conviction of Naser Orić (the ARBiH commander in Srebrenica), having originally held him responsible for crimes ARBiH soldiers had committed against Serbs in June 1992–March 1993. In 2012–13, appeal judges overturned several prominent command-responsibility convictions: Ante Gotovina and Mladen Markač, two Croatian generals originally convicted of crimes against humanity during Oluja; Ramush Haradinaj, Idriz Balaj and Lahi Brahimaj, three ex-Kosovo Liberation Army (KLA) commanders (Haradinaj, who had entered politics, was Kosovo's prime minister when indicted in 2005); and Momčilo Perišić, chief of the Yugoslav Army's general staff after August 1993. Public reactions in post-Yugoslav states to all these appeal results treated the ICTY's individual verdicts as endorsing or rejecting particular narratives about the entire conflict [356; 363: 32–4; 382; 384].

The ICTY, however, was not the only court adjudicating on the wars. Courts in post-Yugoslav states also heard war crimes cases, and one aim of international peacebuilding was to strengthen domestic legal systems' capacity to investigate and try these. The State Court of Bosnia-Herzegovina, supported by the Office of the High Representative (OHR) and ICTY, opened a War Crimes Chamber in 2005. It heard cases under Bosnian, not international, law, though it had mixed panels of Bosnian and foreign judges. Suspects arrested abroad could thereafter be extradited to Bosnia-Herzegovina. In 2011, for instance, Rasema Handanović, whose ARBiH squad had killed 22 Croats in Trusina in April 1993, was arrested in the USA and extradited to Bosnia-Herzegovina, where she was convicted in 2012. Some foreign courts also tried war crimes directly, notably the German court that convicted Nikola Jorgić (a former Serb paramilitary from Doboj) of genocide in 1997 [369: 1207]. The United Nations Mission in Kosovo (UNMIK), meanwhile, supervised war crimes courts in Kosovo.

War crimes trials in Croatia and Serbia, meanwhile, took place within the ordinary criminal justice system. Croatia held its first in 1992, against Serb soldiers and paramilitaries; the state began investigating crimes by Croatian soldiers in 2001, though efforts to prosecute Croats still met with obstruction [353]. The most prominent case heard in Croatia involved Mirko Norac, investigated as a commander for crimes against Serb civilians in Gospić. He was convicted with two associates in 2003, then extradited to the ICTY in 2004 on an indictment concerning the Medak pocket. The ICTY transferred this back to the Croatian courts, which convicted him in 2008. Norac, like Gotovina, had been a focus for protests in Croatia that rejected the ICTY's claim to determine the legitimacy of Croatian actions during the Homeland War [344: 200–26]. Post-Tuđman patriotic musicians, chiefly Marko Perković-Thompson and Miroslav Škoro, joined the campaigns [187]. In Serbia, the gravest war crimes trial heard domestically concerned five paramilitaries (the 'Scorpions' trial) accused of killing Bosniak civilians near Srebrenica in July 1995. ICTY prosecutors showed a video of the executions in June 2005 during Milošević's trial. A Serbian court convicted the five in April 2007, but without fully investigating their links with Serbia's regular police force [375].

Outside the ICTY, the single most significant case about the Yugoslav wars at an international court was the ICJ genocide case that the Bosnian state opened against the Federal Republic of Yugoslavia (FRY) in 1993 [215: 102–9; 337: 111–20]. The defendant state was simply Serbia by the time the ICJ heard evidence in 2006 and gave judgement in 2007. The ICJ ruled that genocide had been committed at Srebrenica in July 1995, and that the FRY authorities had not acted to prevent it, but that the conflict as a whole was not genocidal. Like many ICTY trials, arguments at the ICJ involved the direct opposition of collective historical narratives – the narrative that Milošević as well as Karadžić and Mladić waged a genocidal war against Bosniaks, against the narrative that Bosnian Serbs had been defending themselves in a civil war and Serbia/FRY was not involved [367].

In controversies about the tribunals and judgements, the idea that courts' verdicts on individuals implied broader findings of guilt or innocence put interpretations of the entire conflict at stake. The most extensive controversies concerned ICTY decisions to (not) indict specific people, which lent themselves to inferences about which side the ICTY and its 1999–2008 chief prosecutor Carla del Ponte appeared to hold responsible. In Croatia, Gotovina's supporters often said they were campaigning for 'the truth about the Homeland War': referring to 'the truth' implied that any narrative where the Croatian Army's actions were crimes would be false and that the ICTY should not even have been questioning this [384]. Yet the ICTY was simultaneously being accused of anti-Serb bias, for having indicted more Serbs than anyone else [315: 63]. One controversy surrounded the *absence* of indictments, and this was whether the ICTY should have indicted NATO commanders in 1999 for not distinguishing between military and civilian targets or for using cluster munitions [17: 178–9; 163: 296; 352: 366–7]. These varied arguments shared an expectation that international criminal justice would, if it functioned properly, have produced a single authoritative account of the Yugoslav wars.

Justice and the production of historical narratives

Transitional justice, especially the ICTY's work, relied on historical research into the Yugoslav wars but also facilitated new research. ICTY prosecutors and defendants introduced historical narratives into their arguments, and much ICTY evidence, as well as judgements, became available to historians. Milošević's trial alone involved 46,500 pages of courtroom transcripts and 94,500 pages of evidence [376: 192]. Lawyers and judges selected and evaluated evidence in making arguments; as such, they were producing historical narratives, not just using them [337; 359; 373]. Historical evidence at the ICTY covered not only defendants' own pre-war actions but also longer-term background to the wars.

Prosecutors' strategies for using long-term evidence changed [388]. During the first ICTY case, prosecutors used historical evidence to contextualize the Bosnian conflict for the international judges. The prosecution of Milošević, however, depended directly on proving a particular historical claim, about the long-term continuity of plans to create a 'Greater Serbia' by expelling non-Serbs from targeted territory [387: xvii]. Milošević's prosecutors traced the 'Greater Serbia' objective back to the 1844 Garašanin memorandum (Chapter 1), offering this as proof that Milošević had had the necessary 'special intent' for genocide; Milošević, in response, aggressively questioned the prosecution's expert witness about her interpretation of Serbian nationalism. Because Milošević died, his judges never ruled on whether long-term historical evidence could be used in assessing a defendant's guilt. However, the judgement against Radoslav Brđanin in September 2004 was sceptical about using historical testimony to infer genocidal intent. Brđanin's judges convicted him on other charges, but acquitted him of genocide because they believed the intent to forcibly displace non-Serbs did not necessarily amount to the intent to *destroy* a group (in whole or in part). After Brđanin, the OTP appeared to move towards using expert witnesses to comment on 'microhistory' drawn from captured documents rather than on large-scale historical narratives [388: 130]. Historians were being asked different questions as expert witnesses, but still remained important presences in the trials.

In some trials, scholars with opposed positions in academic literature also became opposed in the courtroom. The Tadić trial featured James Gow and Robert Hayden as prosecution and defence expert witnesses respectively. Tadić's defence wanted to use an argument of Hayden's (that Bosnia-Herzegovina should not have been internationally recognized as a state in April 1992) in order to prove the Bosnian conflict had been an internal civil war and therefore Tadić's 'grave breaches' charges should not apply. Gow, meanwhile, was called to support the case that the Serbian state had been involved [165: 24–5; 366; 388: 72–3]. In a 2010 trial, the defence lawyer for Mićo Stanišić (the RS interior minister) and Stojan Župljanin (a regional RS police chief) included part of Hayden's book as documentary evidence while cross-examining Robert Donia, who had been an expert witness for the prosecution. Scholarly controversies were thus being replayed in a setting where judges had authority to criminally convict an individual and, implicitly, to endorse a particular narrative of the war.

Beyond producing its own historical narratives through verdicts, the ICTY as an evidence-gathering institution also ended up facilitating new research. Some research derived directly from ICTY investigations: Gow's *The Serbian Project and its Adversaries*, for instance, derived from advice he had given the OTP in 1994–98 when it needed to establish jurisdiction over FRY and Yugoslav People's Army (JNA) leaders [165]. In other cases, scholars used evidence released by the ICTY in constructing their own arguments. Josip Glaurdić, for instance, used transcripts of Milošević's intercepted telephone calls in 1991–92 to inform his case that Milošević did 'construct and command' the mechanism of an assault on non-Serbs in Croatia and Bosnia-Herzegovina in order to unify Serbs into a new state [162: 97–8]. Edina Bećirević used exhibits from ICTY trials, such as VRS directives and UN officers' reports, to support her argument that the ICTY should have recognized 'genocidal intent' throughout Radovan Karadžić's war aims [206]. Donia's biography of Karadžić also used the ICTY evidence archive heavily [221]. The ICTY's evidence base could be considered 'a gift to historiography', though this was restricted by the amount of evidence that remained confidential, and by whether and how the publicly-released sources would be archived accessibly [359: 18–19; 385: 73].

Historians using ICTY evidence as sources must, however, consider limitations produced by the trial process. Firstly, lawyers, judges and historians used evidence in inherently different ways [354]. Criminal courts only consider evidence relevant if it helps answer whether defendants were guilty of the crimes on their indictment, whereas historians are also interested in matters of motive, context and structure which a court might not need to hear. Evidence introduced at trial is selected by both sides' lawyers for its value in (dis)proving individual guilt rather than achieving broader historical understanding. Since the ICTY's publicly-released documents were those admitted as prosecution or defence exhibits [359: 18], both sides' selectivity affected what entered the public record.

Historians must also consider how the nature of testimony in criminal trials shapes oral evidence. Lawyers question their own witnesses to make specific points to judges, and cross-examine opposing witnesses in order to undermine their credibility – an especially intimidating process for survivors of violence confronted by leaders who had presided over the atrocities they survived [379; 383: 236–7]. Meanwhile, since most ICTY judges and prosecutors did not speak any ex-Yugoslav languages, translation and interpreting were central in evidence production, and arguments about this sometimes reached the courtroom [361]. Appreciating the histories of ICTY oral and written records was essential as historians conducted new research using them.

'Coming to terms with the past'

Transitional justice theories posited that, for the sake of social peace and regional security, post-war societies needed to 'come to terms with the past' – specifically, with crimes and violence committed by the authorities and armed formations that represented each ethno-national group. The ICTY believed individual criminal accountability would enable a collective reckoning with the past within each ex-Yugoslav nation. In the 2000s, this expectation had political and diplomatic backing, since states' path to joining the EU and NATO could be delayed if those institutions considered they had not co-operated enough with the ICTY. However, the domestic repercussions of co-operation revealed that, even if governments changed their approach to the past, this did not automatically change attitudes throughout society.

'Conditionality' particularly affected Croatia, where Tuđman had eventually been prepared to extradite Bosnian Croats but not implicate Croatia's political/military elites in potential crimes. Ivica Račan, the SDP leader who became prime minister in 2000, reversed Tuđman's non-co-operation to accelerate Croatia's EU accession. However, Croatian Democratic Union (HDZ) and veterans' organizations protested in support of Norac and Gotovina in 2001–2, and the controversy broke up Račan's coalition. When the ICTY indicted Bobetko in September 2002, Račan opposed it. In the meantime, Gotovina had fled, with the Croatian authorities suspected of giving him time to escape. The UK and Dutch governments refused to ratify Croatia's EU accession agreement until Gotovina was arrested in December 2005 (Croatia did not join the EU until 2013, whereas Slovenia had joined in 2004) [374]. HDZ's new leader, Ivo Sanader, who defeated Račan in the 2003 elections, dismayed the further right by co-operating with the ICTY to avoid further sanctions. Conditionality, for Croatia and the whole region, seemed more likely to bring legalistic compliance than wider social transformation [381: 5–8]. Such a transformation would have had to reach as far as public understandings of history and bring people to reassess how they thought about their own wartime experiences; indeed, it could even be said that the West asked members of ex-Yugoslav societies to go further in acknowledging their own complicity in violence than it expected of its own public regarding legacies of colonialism and slavery.

If a prerequisite for reconciliation was developing 'a commonly shared history' [381: 4], that implied the public in each successor state would have to set aside the narratives of collective national victimhood which had emerged before and during the wars. Thinking about how whole societies might confront the past therefore required considering wider social and cultural processes, not just tribunals and governmental politics [315: 68]. Legal evidence and testimony could affect 'social knowledge' about war crimes far beyond the courtroom [337: 247], but court proceedings would only be transformative if people acted, talked and changed their beliefs in response to them. This initially appeared to be happening in Serbia after the Scorpions video (which depicted Serbs killing civilians near Srebrenica), though the effect was short-lived [375]. Time also altered Bosnian survivors' perceptions of war crimes tribunals. Bosniak survivors from Prijedor, for instance, had initially hoped the trials would bring them justice, but became disillusioned with the ICTY's short sentences and the tribunals' failure to change local Serbs' understandings of what had happened in 1992–95 [370]. The deficiencies of trials made truth and reconciliation commissions, which did not need to select evidence to win convictions or disprove guilt, attractive in some quarters.

Even then, simply creating a TRC did not guarantee that it would reopen public knowledge about the past in ways conducive to 'unlearning' collective victimhood narratives. For instance, Vojislav Koštunica's 'Yugoslav Truth and Reconciliation Commission' (established in 2001, and never operational) set out to cover long-term causes of Yugoslavia's disintegration, shifting its focus away from crimes committed by Serbs during the 1990s wars as the TRC-as-reconciliation model would have required [365]. This, however, did not invalidate the TRC concept. In 2008, the civil-society coalition REKOM started campaigning for a TRC which would cover the whole of ex-Yugoslavia and, unlike the ICTY, be victim-oriented [378; 384: 163–4]. REKOM's voice joined those of activists such as Women in Black Serbia, Croatia's Documenta centre, Sarajevo's Research and Documentation Centre and the Serbian human rights campaigners Nataša Kandić and Sonja Biserko: all these campaigners tried to challenge one-sided historical narratives in their own countries which praised their nation's heroic self-defence while obscuring crimes of aggression committed by members of that same nation. Their opponents typically accused them of undermining the nation and promoting foreign political agendas. Except at newsworthy moments, campaigns challenging dominant public narratives about the wars generally struggled to reach wider public consciousness, whereas media reproducing those same dominant narratives occupied public space [315; 339; 370; 384]. This was an obstacle for making societies 'come to terms with' or 'confront' the past, since doing so fully would have required action among the whole of society, not just among people who dedicated themselves to contesting historical narratives in public.

Studies of public attitudes to war crimes often focused on Serbia, since Serbs committed the largest number of crimes during the Yugoslav wars, and achieving widespread public recognition of this in Serbia would be important for reconciliation across the region. Public understanding about the recent past in Serbia is often characterized as 'denial'. Biserko, for instance, considered that, two decades after the wars, Serbia still lacked 'critical self-reflection on its recent past' [125: 313]. Ramet, similarly, argued that Serbs were unwilling to confront 'some of the basic facts of the war' and that their denial amounted to 'nationalist sickness' [29: 501/526]. In contrast, one ethnographic study suggested that in Serbia, troubling knowledge about the wars was more often discussed privately than in public, and came from informal sources (such as personal contacts with ex-soldiers and refugees) more than the media; ethnographic research as well as studies of public documents was therefore necessary to comprehend the making sense of the past [339].

The notion of collective victimhood remained a powerful resource for making political claims in Serbia, to the extent that narratives of people who had experienced the wars differently were often pushed out of public debate. However, this was not a particularly Serbian problem, nor a Serb problem. In Croatia, Bosnia-Herzegovina and Kosovo, too, most public memory and political narrative about the wars still revolved around the idea that one's own nation had been innocent victims of an enemy nation's aggression. These narratives most clearly had factual foundation in the politics of recognition around Srebrenica: forensic, documentary and video evidence left no doubt that Serb soldiers and paramilitaries killed 8,000 men and boys near Srebrenica in July 1995 and did so because they were Bosniaks. The difficulty with collective victimhood narratives was instead that their dominance closed down other, uncomfortable questions, such as the extent to which leaders who were still in power might have profited from illicit wartime activities. Undoubtedly this served the interests of post-war political elites. Understandings of the Yugoslav wars therefore remained fragmented across the successor states. At the same time, however, cultural contacts across post-war borders were vibrant enough that some argued a common Yugoslav culture might yet have survived.

8 Culture and Language During and After the Wars

Although separate national identities did not fade away under Yugoslavia, something that could be called a common Yugoslav culture existed too. Historians of the two Yugoslavias have questioned what that might actually have been: how, for instance, did culture under Tito blend some or all of Yugoslavia's ethnonational cultures together while preserving their distinctiveness? Were any particular national movements unduly strengthened or weakened by royalist or socialist Yugoslavia's cultural policies? Did everyone in Yugoslavia have equal access to participating in a shared Yugoslav culture, whatever that might have been? Were the most meaningful forms of Yugoslav culture in everyday life the same as the forms most often promoted officially? While answers would differ from period to period, the questions would still have been meaningful at any point until Yugoslavia was destroyed. Yet the Yugoslav wars, with their logic of ethnic separation, implied Yugoslavia fragmenting as a common cultural space, not just a political entity.

Ethno-political violence, anthropologists suggest, was aimed at unmaking and remaking its targets' everyday consciousness, convincing them they could never live safely as a minority nation. Evaluating what happened to culture, and even language, during the Yugoslav wars is thus a necessary part of evaluating the impact of ethno-political violence. Scholars of wartime and post-war cultural politics have implicated certain cultural forms (such as sport or 'turbo-folk' music) in nationalism and violence and suggested that some other forms (such as independent cinema or alternative rock) offered means of resistance to cultural separation, building up a 'nationalism/resistance' framework within this field. They have also explored ways through which culture connected people to larger collective identities than the nation. The wider

112

south-east European region, or 'the Balkans', was one such cultural area, but another post-war transnational cultural space was actually the former Yugoslavia itself. A few years after the Yugoslav wars, cultural exchanges across what had become international borders resumed and even started becoming routine. After the wars, this might have seemed paradoxical; but it suggested something of the pre-war South Slav cultural area had survived the creation of separate states around exclusive national programmes. An important precondition, however, was the mutual intelligibility of the languages spoken by people who lived in Croatia, Bosnia-Herzegovina, Serbia and Montenegro, also understood by most Slovenes and Macedonians. The wars' cultural history – a component of their political history – was shaped by a longer history of language and nationhood.

Language politics and the Yugoslav wars

The South Slav nations all have closely-related languages. Defining and differentiating them were always political acts: what made a set of speaking and writing standards its own language, not a dialect of another language, and what should a language's standard version contain? Nineteenth-century nationalist movements standardized 'literary' forms of their national languages so that cultural expression could flourish and eventually so that they could become the official language of a future nation-state. When nation-states were competing to expand, as with late nineteenth-/ early twentieth-century Serbian and Bulgarian nationalisms in Macedonia, they wanted to claim as many speakers of a national language as possible in order to show that the land was populated by, and belonged to, members of that nation. The question of what to name the way someone spoke was already political before Yugoslav unification, but the idea that a nation worthy of its own state should have its own separate language remained important in the 1990s.

The Yugoslav wars' most contentious language politics during the Yugoslav wars surrounded the future of 'Serbo-Croatian', because other matters were more settled. Slovenian was already established as separate before 1918, and socialist Yugoslavia recognized Macedonian as separate too. Other languages spoken in Yugoslavia, such as Hungarian, Albanian and Romani, were not mutually intelligible with South Slav languages; how far their speakers were actually included in Yugoslav culture depended on socio-economic status and on Yugoslav policy towards the language's associated nation. Boundaries between languages were clearer in all these cases than with 'Serbo-Croatian'. This combination of language standards originated in an 1850 decision by the Illyrianist linguists and Vuk Karadžić (the 'Vienna Agreement') to base both the Croatian and Serbian literary languages on the same widely-understood 'štokavian' dialect. They disagreed over whether to consider 'štokavian' speakers Croats or Serbs [86: 27], but the dialect still suited both their interests [393: 225]. 'Štokavian' itself had three variants, commonly distinguished by a particular vowel-sound ('ije', 'e' or more rarely 'i'). Vuk and the Illyrianists chose 'ijekavian', as spoken in Croatia, Bosnia and Herzegovina. The Serbian Orthodox Church, however, preferred 'ekavian', as spoken in Serbia and eastern Bosnia, which became the Kingdom of Serbia's standard [389: 383–4].

Twentieth-century 'Serbo-Croatian' thus had two main variants. Despite some differences in vocabulary, grammar and the tell-tale vowel, nothing seriously impeded understanding between them. Today ijekavian is identified with Croatian and ekavian with Serbian, yet the relationship was once more blurred: not only had Vuk Karadžić preferred ijekavian at Vienna, but the nineteenth-century Croatian writer Ante Starčević, who rejected Yugoslavism or co-operation with Serbs, actually wrote in ekavian himself [409: 426]. The boundaries hardened during the twentieth century. Royalist Yugoslavia had hardened the association between ijekavian/Croatian and ekavian/Serbian to a large enough extent that, when the Independent State of Croatia (NDH) took power in Croatia in 1941, its campaign to 'purify' the Croatian language of Serbian targeted ekavian forms [397: 49]. AVNOJ recognized Croatian and Serbian (plus Slovenian and Macedonian) as separate languages in 1944 [397: 115]. However, this changed after 1945. In 1954, the 'Novi Sad Agreement' between Serbian and Croatian linguists termed ijekavian the 'western variant' and ekavian the 'eastern variant' of the 'Serbo-Croatian' or 'Croato-Serbian' language (it did not call them Croatian and Serbian variants). This agreement was one focus of dissent during the Croatian Spring, and a new grammar for a separate Croatian language was published in 1971. Until the 1990s, the main debate was whether Serbo-Croatian was one language or two. Agendas for separate Bosnian and Montenegrin languages existed, but were not prominent until Bosnian, and later Montenegrin, independence.

Before the wars, language politics were already at issue in the 1980s. Among the Slovenian independence campaigners' grievances – even before the *Mladina* trial – was that federal Yugoslav structures, especially the JNA, marginalized Slovenian as a language. Slovenia's language policy after independence broke with Yugoslav practice: Slovenian was the official language, with minority status for Italian and Hungarian, but no official recognition for Serbo-Croat. Croatia's language policy also made linguistic separation from the Yugoslav past a visible aim, but this separation took much more effort because of the closer relationship between Croatian and Serbian. Tuđman's government reissued the 1971 grammar, basing the new literary standard on it, but public changes to language in Croatia did not stop there. Linguists in 1991–94 revived old Croatian vocabulary which Serbian did not use, and created new words based on medieval roots, stating that Croatian had been suppressed under Yugoslav Communism and could now develop independently. Public libraries removed books in ekavian, or in Cyrillic scripts, from collections on grounds that they were Serbian. Scholars including the Croatian linguist Dubravko Škiljan have argued that the language policy of Tuđman's Croatia symbolically excluded Serbs and their language in order to intensify the ethnic separation between Croats and Serbs [418: 11]; this argument gives pause for reflection on whether it would be appropriate to see exclusivist language policy as an accompaniment to ethnopolitical violence.

Croatia was the most-discussed, but not the only, example of post-Yugoslav linguistic nationalism. Montenegro, after independence in 2006, also witnessed the objective of distinguishing the national language from Serbian by differentiating its standard form. A grammar for Montenegrin, building on 1990s proposals for a separate Montenegrin language, was published in 2010. The Montenegrin manual based the national language on ijekavian (ekavian by then connoting Serbian). It also recommended some ways to distinguish Montenegrin from any other ex-Serbo-Croatian language (proposing two extra letters, ś and ź, for specifically-Montenegrin sounds). The proposal was not even welcomed by everyone who identified as Montenegrins rather than Serbs; nevertheless, it demonstrated linguists were again trying to implement the now-familiar link between language and national sovereignty [198].

In Bosnia-Herzegovina, meanwhile, language politics from Serbia and Croatia intersected with new demands to recognize a separate Bosnian language alongside the independent Bosnian state. During the war, HDZ BiH introduced Croatia's new linguistic standard into areas it controlled. The Republika Srpska authorities, too, exercised linguistic prescriptivism by trying to alter the RS's standard form of Serbian. 'Serbo-Croatian' speakers in western Bosnia generally spoke ijekavian even if they were Serbs, but in 1993 Radovan Karadžić declared ekavian the new standard in imitation of Serbia; the media and public did not respond well [397: 78–83]. Approaches to a separate Bosnian language, meanwhile, differed according to the two competing concepts of Bosnian statehood. If Bosnia-Herzegovina were primarily the nation-state of the Bosniaks, this could suggest its language should be differentiated from Croatian and Serbian by emphasizing Turkish loanwords, symbolizing the Ottoman and Islamic dimension of the Bosniak past. Bosnian state television's language policy turned this way in 1994, when SDA was intensifying Bosniak nationalism [35: 265]. In contrast, if the Bosnian state idea was inherently multi-ethnic, a more suitable linguistic standard would recognize multiple variants equally. As in Montenegro, there was no general agreement on Bosnian's exact form – but if a common 'Serbo-Croatian' language no longer existed, neither 'Serbian' or 'Croatian' appeared suitable names for the language of Bosnia-Herzegovina after a war in which the Serbian and Croatian states had both threatened Bosnian sovereignty.

One might well ask how many languages Serbo-Croatian became during the wars; however, the answer depends on one's criteria for considering two speech systems one language or two. Linguists agree the variants of 'Serbo-Croatian' have retained mutual intelligibility [389; 394; 397]. The hindrance that schools in Croatia and the Federation of Bosnia-Herzegovina did not teach Cyrillic was not severe, since Serbian still used Latin script as well. Changes in vocabulary and grammar were not so drastic that speakers could not adapt, though the alienating effect of the state telling someone that their speech now made them a minority was real. The linguist Ranko Bugarski described the post-war situation as 'one language linguistically but four languages politically', acknowledging the political demands for separate linguistic recognition in the successor states [394: 165]. Bugarski also suggested thinking of the former Serbo-Croatian as one 'polycentric' language, which (as in different English- or Spanish-speaking countries) could contain several standards without undermining any state's sovereignty [394: 165]. Post-war usage found various other solutions. The ICTY used the abbreviation 'BCS' (for 'Bosnian, Croatian and Serbian') and many foreign institutions, even some Bosnian ones, followed its lead [361]. Speakers of the language(s) could simply call it 'our language' (*naš jezik*), and indeed people in the Kingdom of Yugoslavia and even nineteenth-century Croatia had sometimes done that too [393: 225]. The phrase hinted at a sense of cultural similarity that did not imply a need for political unity but had still been shaped by much earlier decisions about language.

Popular culture, ethno-national separation and war

The impact of politics on culture, arts and entertainment during the Yugoslav wars has been extensively documented. In every post-Yugoslav state, but especially those at war, state newspapers and broadcasters amplified political leaders' discourses and symbols, and most non-state-owned mainstream media joined in. While these arguments most often concern news media [21; 35; 39], entertainment media were also involved. As with language policy, the impact of nationalism on popular culture is well seen with Croatia: before independence, and even more so during the war, Croatian anthropologists observed how hundreds of new patriotic pop songs fitted into the symbolic culture of Tuđman's Croatia. The songs drew on the same historical references as political discourse, and got most airplay if they sounded the most 'Western' or 'European' [411]. Croatia's music business had repositioned itself around Croatian nationalism rather than Yugoslav public culture.

Throughout the 1990s, musicians, composers and entertainment journalists differed on how to interpret Croatian national identity but maintained the principle that an independent nation should have its own distinctive popular culture, separate from anything 'Yugoslav' and especially 'Serbian' [187]. Defining national identity depended, in Croatia as elsewhere, on including what should belong but also excluding what should not belong. The reverse side of creating a new patriotic popular culture in the early 1990s was that earlier cultural production became publicly invisible if perceived as Communist, Serbian or Balkan. The author Dubravka Ugrešić called this the 'confiscation of memory', viewing it as a deliberate attempt to reshape public consciousness so that the memory of belonging to Yugoslavia would eventually disappear from people's lives [200: 217].

Popular culture in wartime Bosnia-Herzegovina, where three ethno-national projects and a disempowered multi-ethnic concept opposed each other, presented a more complex and surprisingly rarely studied case. As in Croatia, musicians emphasized sounds and lyrics that symbolized a particular ethno-national culture and produced new songs in explicit or implicit support of each armed force [404]. Bosnian towns' cultural scenes fragmented as members each decided to stay or leave, and anyone who moved to Belgrade was widely seen as taking Milošević's side by those who remained. In these conditions, independent cultural production in besieged cities became a means of resistance to the war and, usually, to nationalism of any kind, including the Bosniak nationalism that ended up prevailing over multi-ethnic Bosnianness in the government and the Army of the Republic of Bosnia-Herzegovina (ARBiH). Participants in wartime Sarajevo's theatre, music, art and radio projects identified with the narrative of Sarajevo's cosmopolitan past and wanted to influence Western governments to intervene on the Bosnian side, but tried to keep themselves separate from the state [237].

Beyond the history of cultural production during the wars, there were also arguments that certain cultural forms, derived from folk culture, *enabled* violence. Just as some authors drew continuities between the Kosovo poems and 1980s–90s Serbian nationalism [2: 190–210; 55], Njegoš's fictional depiction of Serbs massacring Turks in *The Mountain Wreath* – among the most famous epic poems in Serb culture – was accused of creating a worldview which later legitimized extermination of Bosnian Muslims in 1992–95 [206: 43–4; 240: 70; 248: 29–52]. A less deterministic approach explored short-term political uses of folk culture. Eric Gordy, for instance, argued that one way in which

Milošević's regime 'destroyed [political and social] alternatives' during the wars was by promoting a particular kind of popular music, 'turbo folk' [133]. Musically, turbo folk updated the 'newly-composed folk music' developed for the 1950s–80s Yugoslav entertainment media [415]. It combined elements of early-1990s hip hop and dance music with lyrics and vocals intended to sound like traditional folk music. Anti-war cultural commentators in Serbia argued that turbo folk songs and videos glorified a nationalist patriarchal culture by objectifying women and romanticizing organized crime [403]. A later interpretation of turbo folk moved away from the argument that Milošević imposed it on Serbs, linking it to the emergence of very similar pop-folk styles across post-socialist south-east Europe as a whole [390].

The anti-war critique of turbo folk drew on broader arguments that traditional folk culture had become a resource for 1980s–90s nationalist politicians in Serbia and elsewhere in ex-Yugoslavia. Ivan Čolović, writing on Serbia, and Ivo Žanić, writing on Croatia and Bosnia-Herzegovina, both suggested that the value-system of traditional epic poetry from the Dinaric highlands persisted into the 1990s and allowed politicians to tap into collective memory that had been sustained through folklore [130; 424]. Discussing contemporary conflicts in familiar, mythic terms, they suggested, made it easier to persuade the public that war was necessary.

Alongside music, another productive topic for scholars of post-Yugoslav culture and nationalism became sport – and indeed, understanding the Eurovision Song Contest (a site for performing national identity both before and after Yugoslavia's break-up) required some insights into both phenomena. Both music and sport had a key moment that often entered general works on the wars. For music, this was the marriage of the 'turbo folk' singer Ceca Veličković to Arkan in 1995, and for sport it was the football match in Zagreb between Dinamo Zagreb and Red Star Belgrade on 13 May 1990, soon after HDZ had won the Croatian parliamentary elections, which was halted when visiting Red Star fans attacked the Dinamo stands. As the fight escalated, Dinamo's captain Zvonimir Boban was photographed kicking a police officer. Beyond this eye-catching potential starting-point for narratives of the wars [34: 90], more sustained consideration of the wartime role of sport demonstrated how far nationalist politics aimed to reorder social life.

Sport, already 'an efficient instrument of official national-ism' in Tito's Yugoslavia, continued to be so in the post-Yugoslav states [28: 94/207]. Overwhelmingly, sports research has con-centrated on men's football. Čolović, for instance, suggested a direct link between pre-war hooligan groups and paramilitary units like Arkan's, whose first members were Red Star support-ers [130: 259–86]. In Croatia, Tuđman used sport to promote Croatia's separateness from Yugoslavia and his own role in achieving Croatian sovereignty, yet evidence from sport also demonstrated limits to his control over public identity narratives. Tuđman forced Dinamo to change its name to 'Croatia Zagreb' in 1991–93 because 'Dinamo' exemplified Communist cul-ture (paralleling 'confiscations of memory' elsewhere), but the fans' association always resisted this and it quickly reverted after Tuđman's death [188; 191]. Football in Bosnia-Herzegovina, meanwhile, was one of many tools of ethnic separation as the Yugoslav football league disintegrated [242]. During the war, Velež Mostar FC, with a multi-ethnic fan base, was targeted by Croat nationalists who founded an exclusively Croat rival club, Zrinjski. Zrinjski even moved into the Velež stadium, in the part of Mostar claimed by HDZ. The wartime Republic of Serb Krajina (RSK) and RS authorities organized their own sporting federations and leagues as signs of the statehood they claimed, though front-line conditions meant the leagues did not fully function [177]. Other sports were far less studied, and even then it was only men's sport; women's sport remained all but invisible in the sporting history of the wars.

The post-Yugoslav cultural area

During the Yugoslav wars, culture and entertainment became instruments for building ethnically homogenous nations. Removing Serbian songs from Croatian radio archives or under-mining a multi-ethnic football club in Bosnia directly contributed to the objective of forcing ethno-national groups apart; support-ing the ideological order of a regime that was implicated in the wars, as mid-1990s turbo folk music in Serbia was often accused of doing, contributed to war efforts more indirectly. Yet the cultural history of the wars contained just as many examples of cultural production transcending or even challenging the logic of ethnic separation. Pop-folk music itself could be an example: although in Croatia musicians and critics applied the 'turbo folk' label to anything and everything about popular culture they thought should have been left behind with Yugoslavia, Serbian pop-folk retained an enthusiastic Croatian audience, leading to regular moral panics in the mid-2000s Croatian media [187]. Even Ceca Ražnatović, despite her biography, enjoyed a controversial stardom in post-1990s Slovenia and Croatia, the two states whose national identity was supposedly based on difference from more 'Balkan' parts of Yugoslavia [422]. Although Yugoslavia had collapsed as a state and been forced apart as a society, a common cultural economy still existed within the former Serbo-Croatian linguistic area.

Yugoslavia's political fragmentation therefore did not cause complete cultural fragmentation, even though this had been an objective of the wars. One explanation involves the idea of 'post-socialist nostalgia', though 'nostalgia' amalgamated many different responses – from retrospectively looking back at socialist-era welfare or job prospects as more favourable than the post-socialist free market, to affection for vanished aspects of socialist culture or everyday life. Something similar happened in the former East Germany and USSR and in other eastern European states. Nostalgic expression could also be seen after the Yugoslav wars, although its extent and meanings varied widely. Some postwar popular culture deliberately displayed nostalgia for socialist Yugoslavia. In 2005, the famous Sarajevan rock band Bijelo Dugme, who had split in 1988, reunited for concerts in Sarajevo, Zagreb and Belgrade, three capitals of Yugoslav republics and centres of Yugoslav rock culture. In the mid-1980s they had been one of several Sarajevo bands trying to create an 'emotional Yugoslavism' when Yugoslav identity was already in crisis [407: 204]. Their 2005 marketing used socialist Yugoslav iconography to evoke nostalgic memories, but also to sell more tickets and records by doing so [421]. Unofficial souvenirs and even commemorations of Tito could also easily be found. This might have seemed like a legacy of the old socialist leadership cult, but one sociologist suggested something much more knowing was happening: post-Yugoslav nostalgic practices, in his view, consciously constructed a past that had not existed in order to comment on what the present lacked [420].

Meanwhile, the grassroots rebuilding of a post-Yugoslav cultural space had happened more quietly. In the early 2000s it was headline news if pop musicians performed across the Croatian/Serbian border, in either direction; by the late 2000s it was more newsworthy if a musician *refused* to, and only a few held out [187]. The re-establishment of cultural contacts was tentative in the late 1990s but gathered pace after the Milošević and Tuđman regimes ended. By the late 2000s it had become routine, in popular music and cinema. In 1998, Srđan Dragojević's *Rane* (*Wounds*), about Milošević's Belgrade, became the first Serbian film shown in post-war Croatia after the years of separation. Its Croatian distributor subtitled it, pointedly demonstrating Croatian and Serbian as different languages [406: 154–5]. By the mid-2000s, however, enough cultural connections had been re-established for cross-border film distribution to have become normalized [398].

In 2009, Tim Judah used the phrase 'the Yugosphere' to argue that, after the wars, many common social, economic and cultural connections had emerged which did not depend on the political framework of a common state [400]. This extended across the ex-Yugoslav region and into its diasporas, except for most Albanians from Kosovo. They rarely participated in the 'Yugosphere', which depended on shared fluency in the ex-Serbo-Croatian languages, and were more tightly connected to the wider Albanian-speaking cultural area in south-east Europe. Public memory of socialist Yugoslavia in Kosovo was also weaker than anywhere else in ex-Yugoslavia, even Croatia [290]. This was a legacy of the Yugoslav idea having applied to the South Slav peoples specifically, not to all Yugoslavia's inhabitants, and of the discriminatory treatment that Albanians had too often experienced from Yugoslav institutions.

The reconstruction of a 'Yugosphere', or cultural exchange among South Slavs without demands for political unification, implicitly challenged one dynamic of the Yugoslav wars: the assault on Yugoslav togetherness in any form. Beyond this, however, cultural production could also openly critique the wars and their consequences, although creators' opportunities to do so were constrained. Initially, musicians and writers had more scope for critique than film-makers, who depended on state sponsorship. In Serbia, alternative rock bands and the singer-songwriter Đorđe Balašević supported the anti-war protests in 1992, and Balašević used one wartime album to speak out against Serbian aggression and the attack on Vukovar. These were the first Serbian musicians to resume performing in Croatia, in 1998–2000, though ironically they encountered resistance from Croatian music industry bodies [187]. Their music contributed to a transnational, openly anti-nationalist, alternative cultural scene known as the *alternativa* ('alternative'), which celebrated cosmopolitanism, city life and opposition to the political mainstream, while demonstratively rejecting folk culture's 'primitivism' in any form [133; 324]. Expressing cultural tastes helped bind this community together. By the mid-2000s, hip-hop also belonged to this anti-nationalist milieu, and Bosnian rappers such as Edo Maajka, Frenki and Dubioza Kolektiv arguably criticized corruption, nationalism and privatization more harshly than most Bosnian politicians [408].

The costs of critique could, however, be high, especially during the wars. In wartime Croatia, five feminist writers (Slavenka Drakulić, Dubravka Ugrešić, Jelena Lovrić, Vesna Kesić and Rada Iveković) were heavily criticized in the national press after publishing works that criticized the ideological conformity being demanded from Croatia's citizens. After the so-called 'Croatian witches' scandal, Drakulić and Ugrešić both left Croatia. They, like Aleksandar Hemon (who stayed in the USA after the siege of Sarajevo broke out during his studies), were widely translated into English and celebrated as exile writers. Western archetypes of dissidents and refugees made their books easy to promote, but this framework dominated English-language publishing so much that it affected the translation prospects of authors who did not write about human rights or war [412].

1990s post-Yugoslav film-making, meanwhile, was less politically engaged than the self-consciously alternative wings of literature or popular music. 1990s films often either re-stated their country's dominant narratives about the war and the national past or depicted the wars exotically as the latest incarnation of an endemic cycle of Balkan violence (as with mid-1990s films by Emir Kusturica, Srđan Dragojević and Milčo Mančevski) [399; 410]. In reaction, some 2000s film-makers used social realism to provoke greater reflection among audiences [410]. Bosnian cinema provided the most examples, spurred on by the international success of Danis Tanović's *Ničija zemlja* (*No Man's Land*), a 2001 satire of the Bosnian war and UN peacekeeping. Films by two Bosnian women, Jasmila Žbanić and Aida Begić, depicted the combined effects of the war and the collapse of socialism on Bosnian society. Žbanić's 2006 film *Grbavica* (*Esma's Secret*) publicized the subject of war rape. *Grbavica* was critically acclaimed abroad, and won the 2006 Berlin Film Festival. This victory was celebrated in the Federation as a national success, but in terms reinforcing Bosniaks' collective victimhood, which had not been Žbanic's theme [318: 209–10].

The Balkans and south-east Europe: history across borders?

The cultural aftermath of the Yugoslav wars demonstrated political separation would not permanently isolate South Slavs from each other culturally. The new 'Yugosphere' spread unevenly and could encounter resistance; it was not a simple reintegration or restoration, but a reconfiguration of what had existed before. It rested on the longer-term idea of 'South Slavs' as a group of peoples who, even if they formed separate nations that would exercise political self-determination independently, still had something in common that was not shared with other neighbours. This wider cultural 'Yugoslav idea' outlasted twentieth-century attempts at implementing it politically. In some accounts, however, even the nineteenth century would be too late a starting-point for explaining the 'Yugosphere'. It might equally relate to even longer-term cultural legacies within the Balkans – though one first had to clarify what 'the Balkans' could mean. Simplistic explanations ascribing the Yugoslav wars to a 'Balkan' capacity for violence obscured the conflicts' political dimensions (and since nowhere in the Balkan peninsula outside ex-Yugoslavia was involved, they certainly did not deserve being called the 'Balkan wars' in English [419: 186]). However, more nuanced considerations of south-east Europe as a cultural area could help explain why one section of it, the 'Yugosphere', turned out more resilient than might have been expected. The history of 'the Balkans' as an idea also helps to explain the construction of post-Yugoslav national identities during the wars themselves.

During the Yugoslav wars, ideas of 'the Balkans' themselves became a topic for scholarly research. Milica Bakić-Hayden and Maria Todorova both started with the idea that 'the Balkans' and 'Europe' were often represented as each other's opposites

[391; 419]. They agreed that, inside and outside south-east Europe, a hierarchy of stereotypes appeared to associate 'Europe' with modernity and civilization and 'the Balkans' with primitivism and backwardness. Bakić-Hayden, writing with Robert Hayden, argued that Slovenian and Croatian nationalist arguments in 1988–91 had supported their cases for independence with a historical narrative that Yugoslavia, especially Serbia, belonged to the Balkans whereas Slovenia and Croatia were European [108]. Later, she argued these representations 'nested' inside each other: Croatian identity might be based on Europeanness, but from Slovenia's viewpoint Croatia seemed 'Balkan' itself [391]. Todorova also engaged with the European/Balkan opposition but focused on the nineteenth-century 'imagining' of the Balkans from outside, by western European travellers [419]. Both scholars were influenced by Edward Said's *Orientalism*, which argued that nineteenth-century Europeans had invented the image of an exotic 'Orient' to legitimize imperial rule over the Middle East.

Though Todorova and Bakić-Hayden differed in how they related their own arguments to Said's, their work opened up more research on so-called 'Balkanism' [44]. Vesna Goldsworthy, for instance, suggested fictional representations of the Balkans were as important as purportedly-factual ones in constructing 'Balkanist' stereotypes [395]. The 1990s wars and their aftermath produced ever more material for studying 'Balkanism'. One study of 1990s Croatia, for instance, demonstrated that Croatians with very different political positions – not only Tuđman, but also liberal democrats and anti-nationalist activists – all used ideas of 'Europe' versus 'the Balkans', though gave the concepts different meanings depending on their own political agendas [199]. Images of the Balkans were not uniformly negative; by the early 2000s, south-east European popular culture was already exhibiting a trend for *celebrating* the Balkans as an irrational, hedonistic place [401]. Films, musicians and books that fitted existing Western expectations of the Balkans were also more likely to sell well abroad, and this economic incentive contributed to what Dina Iordanova termed 'consenting self-exoticism' within the region [399: 56]. The continuing Western appetite for Balkan exotica fed off how the 1990s wars had been reported.

Stereotypes aside, there was some truth to the idea that south-east European national cultures had something distinctive in common. Indeed, different national cultures frequently had competing claims over the same symbols and myths: Ivo Žanić's study of 'hajduk' (bandit) mythology, for instance, found that 1990s epic poets praised their Croat or Serb national heroes in extremely similar terms, even though Croatian and Serbian nationalisms were then directly opposed [424]. Likewise, the same song melodies commonly existed in several south-east European languages, inside and outside ex-Yugoslav space. The film-maker Adela Peeva, researching her 2003 documentary *Chia e tazi pesen?* (*Whose Is This Song?*), located Turkish, Greek, Bulgarian, Albanian, Bosnian, Serbian and Macedonian adaptations of the same Sephardic and Ottoman folk-song, and her evidence it also 'belonged' to other nations did not go down well with some interviewees [392]. Contemporary south-east European pop-folk songs were similarly liable to be translated into several languages, whether acknowledged by composers or not.

Much of south-east Europe's shared cultural heritage could be attributed to customs and traditions that emerged before the region had been divided into nation-states, and especially under Ottoman rule. Indeed, Donna Buchanan called the south-east European cultural region the 'Ottoman ecumene', that is, a space of intentional cultural interchange across national and religious borders [392: xx]. The explanation, however, avoided determinism. Although an 'Ottoman ecumene' could certainly be observed in post-socialist south-east Europe, Buchanan attributed it not just to shared Ottoman history but also to the extensive role of Romani musicians (who regularly crossed national borders for work) and to the expansion of a transnational music market in south-east Europe after the collapse of socialism, when musicians could no longer count on the same patronage from the state [392: xviii–xix]. Building on these insights, one historian of music in south-east Europe asked: 'How can we denationalize music histories?' [416: 660]. Historians of any topic, not just music, could benefit from asking this question, since automatically choosing a specific nation as one's unit of analysis could obscure developments that are difficult to study through a single national lens. Scholars of music in south-east Europe, for instance, did better than scholars of most other topics in making visible the experiences of Roma, who were marginalized to the point of invisibility in studies of the Yugoslav wars [343; 417].

How far, however, could the project of 'denationalizing' history go when writing about the Yugoslav wars, when people were killed, tortured and forced from their homes because of what ethno-national group they belonged or were assigned to? Ethno-political violence reduced its victims to an ethnic label, which made them enemies and less than human in their killers' and captors' eyes. However, recognizing that this occurred did not mean one must accept the aggressors' framing of the conflict as a war between ethnic groups that could not live together. The post-war history of language and culture in former Yugoslavia went some way to demonstrating that the South Slavs, at least, did not belong to such separate cultures as the leaders who commanded attacks wanted to believe. The extent of the assault on national ambiguity during the Yugoslav wars meant that, to assess their outcome, one must look to culture and the everyday as well as politics.

The scope of this history of the Yugoslav wars has widened out from the questions of guilt and responsibility with which it began when it assessed the 1980s crisis, Milošević's forcible reshaping of the federation, and the independence of Slovenia, Croatia and Bosnia-Herzegovina. Those questions remain essential, and newly-available sources enable scholars to answer them with ever more precision. However, historians were also able to address aspects of the wars which are not so easily contained within the task of weighing up guilt but which are still valuable for understanding the recent past. They could explore the social and economic inequalities that the wars perpetuated, transformed or created anew, and they could return to visibility the alternative structures of solidarity, action and thought that were defeated in the build-up to war. Ultimately, they could show that histories of the wars and of the collapse of Yugoslav socialism deserved to be interdependent.

Conclusion

The history of the Yugoslav wars cannot be detached from the collapse of Yugoslav socialism as an economic and political system. The crises that affected ever more dimensions of society by the mid-1980s created new opportunities for individuals and interest-groups to attempt radical transformations of the federation. By 1989, new Party leaders in Serbia and Slovenia had two fundamentally-incompatible programmes: Milošević's programme to recentralize the federation around Serbia at the expense of other republics' and provinces' autonomy, and Kučan's programme to decrease federal control so that republics could pursue more independent courses. In terms of how Milošević and Kučan communicated with the publics they addressed, and even how they played on nationalism in doing so, the programmes were comparable; they differed, however, in the level of military force available to them and the ways in which they were prepared to use it. The Yugoslav People's Army (JNA), whose generals found common ground with Milošević, made itself available to the federal government for opposing the secession of 'subversive' Slovenia, but no federal structure was strong enough to order it to change course and act against Milošević's destabilizing activities, including the support he gave through Serbian security services to the Serb Democratic Party militias in Croatia and Bosnia-Herzegovina. Ultimately, these activities proved even more ominous for the federation, since they compelled the Croatian and Bosnian authorities to prepare for war.

Today's historians can assess the Yugoslav wars as the destruction of a state, which had controlled material resources and mechanisms of power; an idea, which had implied that the South Slav nations should form a cultural and a political community; and a society, in which the lives of 23 million people were disrupted even more radically than they could have imagined when the last Yugoslav crisis began [7]. In these conflicts, nationalism was more an instrument than a cause: the histories of nationalism in general and of the ex-Yugoslav (including Albanian) national-ist movements in particular were preconditions for the course of each post-Yugoslav war, yet it was not predetermined which con-cepts of national identity or national interests would prevail or what those contestations' material implications would be. The break-up of Yugoslavia involved the defeat of alternative out-comes, both within each republic and at the federal level, and the closing-down of non-ethno-national political communities. In this sense, a 'war on ambiguity' occurred before and during the armed conflicts, and indeed it suited the successor states' post-war elites to continue defining political and social problems in the same nationalist terms. For some time the ethnic and national dimen-sions of the wars also shaped scholars' interpretive frameworks, although in the 2000s an increasing number were writing against this frame.

The Yugoslav wars were wars of ethno-political separation, fought with the aim of creating nation-states in which one ethnically-defined nation would form the basis of the political community. Visions of a national community with a shared cul-tural past which did not depend on ethnicity were stronger on the Sarajevo government side than on any other, though by the end of the Bosnian conflict even these had been politically mar-ginalized at the top level of government by Bosniak nationalism. Yet recognizing that the dominant political programmes in the Yugoslav wars all depended on the primacy of ethno-nationalism, and acknowledging that this ideology excluded ethnic 'others' from the national community, does not mean that equal respon-sibility would fall on all sides where exclusivist nationalism could be seen. Primary responsibility lies with those who ordered and committed acts of aggression. While the post-Yugoslav conflicts were wars about ethno-political separation, they were also wars of opportunism and control: the further historians research the micro-dynamics of conflict in and behind the frontline areas, the more evidence for them also having been wars of material enrichment is likely to emerge, and the field would benefit in particular from a systematic and transnational study of organized crime.

While the war in Slovenia concerned locations of state power (the republic's border posts and ports of entry), the wars in Croatia, Bosnia-Herzegovina and Kosovo targeted the human fabric of villages and towns. Several valuable studies have suggested that the most productive levels for studying the Yugoslav wars in coming years may therefore be municipal or microhistorical – approaches that have already helped demonstrate the social and political complexity of the Spanish Civil War and the Russian Revolution. Studying how the Serb Democratic Party gained control of the municipalities around Knin in 1990–91, or how civic activists in Tuzla forged networks that kept nationalist parties out of local government in 1991–95, illustrates the dynamics of the conflict in important ways [166; 205]. This level of detail is also necessary to prove the point that collective memories and national narratives do not, on their own, cause wars: scholars must strive to understand how memories, narratives and ideas have been translated into social and political action [328]. This book has introduced several types of question that have become essential to consider in understanding the Yugoslav wars. Some are about complicity and culpability; some are about the history of nationalism and this political idea's material consequences; some are about the effects of the collapse of Yugoslav socialism, a system that had structured society and managed the economy.

The question of whether or not it is possible to produce one single authoritative narrative of the Yugoslav wars that will satisfy all parties still divides scholars. Sabrina Ramet argues that historians should 'go behind the interpretations and seek out [...] the truth' through careful recourse to the facts about reality [52: 51]. Josip Glaurdić emphasizes that the most accurate interpretations are those best grounded in primary sources [45: 34–5]. With time and persistence, scholars have indeed been able to establish more detailed accounts about aspects of the wars: for instance, more precision is available now than ten years ago about the number of Bosnian war dead, or the timescale for the takeover by the Serb Democratic Party (SDS) of the Croatian and Bosnian municipalities it targeted. Yet as early as 1998, David Campbell suggested, after comparing how ten mid-1990s books presented 32 political events of 1990–2 in Bosnia-Herzegovina, that 'it is perhaps beyond the capacity of any single narrative to provide the best account' [215: 281]. He proposed instead that one could best gain a full understanding of the past through comparing competing narratives against each other.

Two decades after the Yugoslav wars, understanding their history requires attention to the evidence but also appreciation of how they have been interpreted before. Interpretations and narratives are part of the past, not separate from it, and they themselves are open to historical study and critique: indeed, even the most empiricist historians must sort and arrange evidence in the course of communicating their work. Understanding how and why a historical narrative takes the shape it does is important for appreciating how historical knowledge about the Yugoslav wars has been produced; but 'deconstructing' history in this sense is not the same as, and should not be used for, excusing the denial of what can be established firmly. Nor should it become abstract theorizing about real lives and deaths.

This volume has aimed to introduce readers to scholarly interpretations of the Yugoslav wars as they stand in the scholarly literature currently published in or translated into English – the body of work that most readers of this series will have access to. The work of comparing published interpretations of the wars began in their immediate aftermath, when Sarah Kent noted: 'The nearer we are to the unfolding of an event, the harder it is to determine which witnesses best represent what historians will eventually identify as the dominant trends' [50: 1113]. In fact, new trends would emerge instead, as multiple scholars in the 2000s aimed to write against 'history in the national mode' [41: 150]. Collective narratives about the past and present, especially those revolving around victimhood, came under increasing scrutiny, in recognition that even the most emancipatory of collective narratives might silence aspects of the past [318]. In the 2010s, socio-economic questions about the causes and consequences of the Yugoslav wars became more urgent after the post-2008 global financial crisis [320], and an even more explicit 'history across borders' emerged in research on the pre-1918 region, with implications for historicizing twentieth-century ethno-nationalist territorial claims. With the effects of the 1990s wars nonetheless remaining social facts however much one deconstructed the categories of 'nationalism' and 'ethnicity', a new archival turn promised ever greater clarity about participants and events. Yet important aspects of the wars, for instance the history of peace activism in the region or the interdependence of the dynamic of warfare with the collapse of socialism, could not be answered solely through research agendas that were about determining guilt. Moreover, certain topics – such as the history of organized crime, or 1990s relationships between the ex-Yugoslav region and the non-Western world – still remained almost unexplored. Throughout these turns, the need to compare and critically evaluate interpretations remained.

Timeline (1980–2000)

1980

4 May   Death of Josip Broz Tito

1981

March–May   Protests by Albanians in Kosovo

1986

May   Milan Kučan becomes Party leader in Slovenia
                  Slobodan Milošević becomes president of
                  Serbia's Central Committee
24 September   'Serbian Academy of Arts and Sciences'
                  memorandum leaked

1987

January   'Contributions for a Slovenian National
                  Programme' published
24 April   Milošević visits Kosovo Polje
September   'Agrokomerc' scandal revealed in
                  Bosnia-Herzegovina
                  Milošević forces resignation of Ivan Stambolić

1988

May	*Mladina* leaks case in Slovenia
September	Milošević's 'anti-bureaucratic revolution' demonstrations begin
October	Party leaders in Vojvodina resign

1989

11 January	Party leaders in Montenegro resign
January	'Association for a Yugoslav Democratic Initiative' (UJDI) founded
February	Kosovo miners' strike resisting revocation of Kosovo's autonomy
	Kučan addresses Slovenian support rally for Kosovo
16 March	Ante Marković becomes federal prime minister
28 March	Republic of Serbia revokes autonomy of Vojvodina and Kosovo
28 June	Milošević's 600th anniversary Kosovo speech
July	Slovenian constitutional amendments proposed
13 December	Ivica Račan becomes Party leader in Croatia
23 December	Democratic League of Kosovo (LDK) founded

1990

22 January	Slovenian and Croatian delegates leave Party congress
17 February	Serb Democratic Party (SDS) founded in Croatia
24–25 February	Croatian Democratic Union (HDZ) holds first congress
27 March	Party of Democratic Action (SDA) founded in Bosnia-Herzegovina
8–22 April	Slovenian elections (DEMOS controls parliament; Kučan president)

22 April–6 May	HDZ wins Croatian elections
May	Yugoslav People's Army (JNA) disarms Slovenian/Croatian Territorial Defence
30 May	HDZ founder Franjo Tuđman becomes president of Croatia
17 June	VMRO–DPMNE (nationalist party) founded in Macedonia
July	Marković founds 'Association of Reformist Forces of Yugoslavia'
12 July	Serb Democratic Party (SDS) founded in Bosnia-Herzegovina
25 July	'Serb National Council' in Croatia calls for referendum on autonomy
17 August	SDS roadblocks against Croatian police in Knin ('log revolution')
18 August	HDZ founds Bosnian branch
30 September	'Serb Autonomous Region of Krajina' declared
October	Slovenian–Croatian 'confederation' proposal
November	Macedonian elections (VMRO–DPMNE first, ex-Communists second)
	SDA, HDZ and SDS form coalition after Bosnian elections
December	Socialist Party of Serbia (SPS) wins Serbian elections
23 December	Slovenian independence referendum

1991

January	Federal parliament discusses disarming Croatia
February	Slovenia declares intent to secede
	Izetbegović-Gligorov 'asymmetric federation' proposal
9 March	Large anti-Milošević demonstrations in Belgrade
25 March	Milošević and Tuđman meet at Karađorđevo
March	SDA forms 'Patriotic League'

March–May	Confrontations between Croatian police and JNA
April–May	Croatian 'National Guard' (ZNG) formed
2 May	Borovo Selo massacre
19 May	Croatian independence referendum
25 June	Croatia and Slovenia declare independence
27 June–3 July	JNA operations against Slovenia
3–5 July	JNA advances into Croatia
7 July	Brioni Agreement
July	'Centre for Anti-War Action' founded in Belgrade
July–September	JNA offensive escalates in eastern Slavonia and Krajina
27 August	EC forms 'Badinter Commission'
8 September	Macedonian independence referendum
14 September	ZNG starts attacking JNA barracks in Croatia
23 September	JNA attack on Dubrovnik begins
25 September	Macedonia declares independence
September	SDS in Bosnia-Herzegovina declares 'Serb Autonomous Regions'
8 October	Brioni Agreement moratorium expires
October	SDS withdraws from Bosnian parliament, forms own assembly
	'Women in Black' founded in Belgrade
18 November	JNA captures Vukovar
19 December	SDS in Croatia declares 'Republic of Serb Krajina' (RSK)
	SDS in Bosnia-Herzegovina sends 'crisis headquarters' plans

1992

2 January	'Sarajevo Ceasefire' between Croatia and JNA
9 January	SDS in Bosnia-Herzegovina declares sovereign 'Republika Srpska' (RS)
15 January	EC recognizes Slovenia and Croatia

February–March 'Cutileiro Plan' negotiations

21 February United Nations Protection Force (UNPROFOR) sent to Croatia

1 March Bosnian independence referendum, boycotted by SDS

SDS temporarily barricades Sarajevo streets

18 March 'Lisbon Agreement' signed

31 March Serbian police and paramilitaries begin attack in eastern Bosnia

5 April Serb snipers fire on Sarajevo peace demonstration

6 April Bosnia-Herzegovina declares independence

8 April Croat Defence Council (HVO) formalized

15 April Army of the Republic of Bosnia-Herzegovina (ARBiH) formed

27 April Serbia/Montenegro become 'Federal Republic of Yugoslavia' (FRY)

30 April SDS takeover of Prijedor begins

2 May JNA attempts to divide Sarajevo

3 May 'Dobrovoljačka Street' incident in Sarajevo

4 May Army of Republika Srpska (VRS) formed; continues to attack targeted towns and villages

6 May 'Graz Agreement' between Bosnian SDS and HDZ

12 May Radovan Karadžić's 'six strategic goals' speech

27 May 'Breadline massacre' in Sarajevo

30 May UN introduces sanctions against FRY

29 June UNPROFOR given mandate to secure Sarajevo airport

Early August Western media reports on RS concentration camps

25 August Sarajevo library shelled

26–27 August London Conference on Former Yugoslavia

14 September UNPROFOR to protect aid convoys in Bosnia-Herzegovina

9 October UN declares 'no-fly zone' over Bosnia-Herzegovina

23 October HVO attack on Prozor

1993

2 January	Draft 'Vance–Owen Plan' published
31 March	UN allows NATO enforcement mechanism for no-fly zone
16 April	Srebrenica declared UN 'Safe Area'
	HVO attack on Ahmići
6 May	UN declares Bihać, Goražde, Sarajevo, Tuzla, Žepa 'Safe Areas'
9 May	HVO attack on eastern Mostar (to January 1994)
20 August	'Owen–Stoltenberg Plan' published
27 September	Fikret Abdić declares 'Autonomous Province of Western Bosnia'
9 November	HVO destroys Mostar's 'Old Bridge'
November	In Sarajevo, ARBiH disarms gangster brigades and assimilates HVO

1994

5 February	First 'Markale massacre' in Sarajevo
1 March	ARBiH and HVO sign 'Washington Agreement'
April	VRS attacks Goražde, UN/NATO use air-strikes
Autumn	ARBiH offensives in Bihać pocket

1995

1–3 May	Croatian 'Operation Flash' against RSK
25 May	'Youth Day' VRS artillery attack on Tuzla
28 May	VRS takes UNPROFOR hostages at Goražde
8–10 July	VRS attacks Srebrenica
11–13 July	VRS and paramilitaries kill 8,000 men and boys from Srebrenica
25 July	VRS captures Žepa
4–8 August	Croatian 'Operation Storm' against RSK (entering Knin 8 August)

28 August	Second 'Markale massacre' in Sarajevo
November	Milošević, Tuđman and Izetbegović negotiate in Dayton
14 December	General Framework for Peace in Bosnia-Herzegovina

1996

February	First operations by Kosovo Liberation Army (KLA)
March	RS evacuates Sarajevo suburbs being transferred to Federation
17 November	Protests in Serbia (to February 1997) after local elections

1998

Spring	Serbian security forces begin offensive against KLA (to June 1999)
24 October	UN calls for ceasefire in Kosovo

1999

15 January	Račak massacre
6 February	Rambouillet talks begin
18 March	NATO ultimatum to Milošević to sign the Rambouillet Agreement
24 March	NATO air-strikes against FRY begin (to 9 June)
27 May	International Criminal Tribunal for the Former Yugoslavia (ICTY) indicts Milošević
9 June	Milošević agrees Kosovo to be put under UN administration
	NATO ground troops enter Kosovo
10 December	Franjo Tuđman dies

2000

| September | Vojislav Koštunica defeats Milošević in FRY presidential elections |
| 5 October | Demonstrations in Belgrade, Milošević resigns |

Bibliography

General works

[1] J. B. Allcock, *Explaining Yugoslavia* (London, 2000).

[2] M. Almond, *Europe's Backyard War: The War in the Balkans* (London, 1994).

[3] *Balkan Battlegrounds: A Military History of the Yugoslav Conflict, 1990–1995* (Washington DC, 2002). Detailed operational history by CIA analysts.

[4] *Balkan Battlegrounds: A Military History of the Yugoslav Conflict, 1990–1995* (Washington DC, 2003). Annexes to [3].

[5] C. Bennett, *Yugoslavia's Bloody Collapse: Causes, Course and Consequences* (London, 1994).

[6] L. Benson, *Yugoslavia: A Concise History* (Basingstoke, 2002).

[7] F. Bieber et al., *Debating the End of Yugoslavia* (Farnham, 2014). Spotlights emerging research areas.

[8] L. J. Cohen, *Broken Bonds: Yugoslavia's Disintegration and Balkan Politics in Transition* (Boulder, 1995).

[9] L. J. Cohen and J. Dragović-Soso (eds), *State Collapse in South-Eastern Europe: New Perspectives on Yugoslavia's Disintegration* (West Lafayette, 2008).

[10] M. Crnobrnja, *The Yugoslav Drama*, 2nd ed. (London, 1996).

[11] B. Denitch, *Ethnic Nationalism: The Tragic Death of Yugoslavia*, rev. ed. (Minneapolis, 1996).

[12] D. Djokić (ed.), *Yugoslavism: Histories of a Failed Idea 1918–1992* (London, 2003).

[13] A. Finlan, *The Collapse of Yugoslavia 1991–1999* (Oxford, 2004). Aimed at peacekeepers.

[14] V. P. Gagnon, Jr., *The Myth of Ethnic War: Serbia and Croatia in the 1990s* (Ithaca, 2004). Anti-essentialist.

[15] M. Glenny, *The Balkans 1804–1999: Nationalism, War and the Great Powers* (London, 1999).

[16] M. Glenny, *The Fall of Yugoslavia*, 2nd ed. (London, 1993).

[17] R. M. Hayden, *Blueprints for a House Divided: The Constitutional Logic of the Yugoslav Conflicts* (Ann Arbor, 2000).

[18] M. A. Hoare, 'The War of Yugoslav Succession', in Ramet (ed.), *Central and Southeast European Politics Since 1989*, cited in [30].

[19] K. Hudson, *Breaking the South Slav Dream: The Rise and Fall of Yugoslavia* (London, 2003). Example of Marxist approach.

[20] C. Ingrao and T. A. Emmert (eds), *Confronting the Yugoslav Controversies: A Scholars' Initiative* (West Lafayette, 1st ed. 2009, 2nd ed. 2012). Attempts to collaboratively synthesize one agreed narrative.

[21] K. Kurspahić, *Prime Time Crime: Balkan Media in War and Peace* (Washington DC, 2003).

[22] J. R. Lampe, *Yugoslavia as History: Twice There Was A Country*, 2nd ed. (Cambridge, 2000).

[23] D. B. MacDonald, *Balkan Holocausts? Serbian and Croatian Victim-Centred Propaganda and the War in Yugoslavia* (Manchester, 2002). On disputes about atrocities.

[24] B. Magaš, *The Destruction of Yugoslavia: Tracking the Break-Up 1980–92* (London, 1993). Collects contemporaneous writings.

[25] B. Magaš and I. Žanić (eds), *The War in Croatia and Bosnia-Herzegovina, 1991–1995* (London, 2001). Contributions by several senior Croatian/Bosnian participants.

[26] V. Meier, *Yugoslavia: A History of its Demise*, trans. S. P. Ramet (London, 1999). Useful for 1980s federal politics.

[27] A. Pavković, *The Fragmentation of Yugoslavia: Nationalism and War in the Balkans*, 2nd ed. (Basingstoke, 2000).

[28] V. Perica, *Balkan Idols: Religion and Nationalism in Yugoslav States* (Oxford, 2002).

[29] S. P. Ramet, *The Three Yugoslavias: State-Building and Legitimation, 1918–2005* (Washington DC, 2006). Compare vs. [38].

[30] S. P. Ramet (ed.), *Central and Southeast European Politics since 1989* (Cambridge, 2010). Textbook.

[31] S. P. Ramet and L. S. Adamovich (eds), *Beyond Yugoslavia: Politics, Economics and Culture in a Shattered Community* (Boulder, 1995).

[32] L. Sekelj, *Yugoslavia: the Process of Disintegration*, trans. V. Vukelić (Boulder, 1993).

[33] L. Sell, *Slobodan Milosevic and the Destruction of Yugoslavia* (Durham NC, 2002).

[34] L. Silber and A. Little, *The Death of Yugoslavia*, rev. ed. (London, 1996). Based on extensive interviews.

[35] M. Thompson, *Forging War: Media in Serbia, Croatia and Bosnia-Herzegovina*, 2nd ed. (Luton, 1999).

[36] J. Udovički and J. Ridgeway (eds), *Burn This House: The Making and Unmaking of Yugoslavia* (Durham NC, 1997).

[37] F. Wilmer, *The Social Construction of Man, the State, and War: Identity, Conflict, and Violence in the Former Yugoslavia* (London, 2002).

[38] S. Woodward, *Balkan Tragedy: Chaos and Dissolution after the Cold War* (Washington DC, 1995). Compare vs. [29].

[39] D. Žarkov, *The Body of War: Media, Ethnicity, and Gender in the Break-Up of Yugoslavia* (Durham NC, 2007).

Historiography

[40] I. Banac, 'The Dissolution of Yugoslav Historiography', in Ramet and Adamovich (eds), *Beyond Yugoslavia*, cited in [31].

[41] W. Bracewell, 'The End of Yugoslavia and New National Histories', *European History Quarterly*, vol. 29, no. 1 (1999), pp. 149–56.

[42] D. Djordjevich, 'Clio Amid the Ruins: Yugoslavia and its Predecessors in Recent Historiography', in N. M. Naimark and H. Case (eds), *Yugoslavia and Its Historians: Understanding the Balkan Wars of the 1990s* (Stanford, 2003). On long-term explanations.

[43] J. Dragović-Soso, 'Why Did Yugoslavia Disintegrate?: An Overview of Contending Explanations', in Cohen and Dragović-Soso (eds), *State Collapse in South-Eastern Europe*, cited in [9]. Overview to mid-2000s.

[44] K. E. Fleming, 'Orientalism, the Balkans, and Balkan Historiography', *American Historical Review*, vol. 4, no. 105 (2000), pp. 1218–33.

[45] J. Glaurdić, 'Yugoslavia's Dissolution: Between the Scylla of Facts and the Charybdis of Interpretation', in Bieber et al. (eds), *Debating*, cited in [7]. On value of primary sources.

[46] J. Gow, 'After the Flood: Literature on the Context, Causes and Course of the Yugoslav War: Reflections and Refractions', *Slavonic and East European Review*, vol. 75, no. 3 (1997), pp. 446–84.

[47] M. A. Hoare, 'Genocide in the Former Yugoslavia: A Critique of Left Revisionism's Denial', *Journal of Genocide Research*, vol. 5, no. 4 (2003), pp. 543–63.

[48] S. Jansen, 'National Numbers in Context: Maps and Stats in Representations of the Post-Yugoslav Wars', *Identities*, vol. 12, no. 1 (2005), pp. 45–68. Contextualizes population maps.

[49] D. Jović, 'The Disintegration of Yugoslavia: A Critical Review of Explanatory Approaches', *European Journal of Social Theory*, vol. 4, no. 1 (2001), pp. 101–20. Overview through 1990s.

[50] S. A. Kent, 'Writing the Yugoslav Wars: English-Language Books on Bosnia (1992–1996) and the Challenges of Analyzing Contemporary History', *American Historical Review*, vol. 102, no. 4 (1997), pp. 1085–114.

[51] R. Lindsey, 'From Atrocity to Data: Historiographies of Rape in Former Yugoslavia and the Gendering of Genocide', *Patterns of Prejudice*, vol. 36, no. 4 (2002), pp. 59–78.

[52] S. P. Ramet, 'Disputes about the Dissolution of Yugoslavia and its Wake', in Bieber et al. (eds), *Debating*, cited in [7].

[53] S. P. Ramet, *Thinking About Yugoslavia: Scholarly Debates about the Yugoslav Breakup and the Wars in Bosnia and Kosovo* (Oxford, 2005).

[54] G. Stokes et al., 'Instant History: Understanding the Wars of Yugoslav Succession', *Slavic Review*, vol. 55, no. 1 (1996), pp. 136–60.

Historical background

[55] B. Anzulović, *Heavenly Serbia: From Myth to Genocide* (London, 1999). Cultural determinism.

[56] P. Ballinger, *History in Exile: Memory and Identity at the Borders of the Balkans* (Princeton, 2002). On Italian refugees from Istria/Dalmatia.

[57] P. Ballinger, 'History's "Illegibles": National Indeterminacy in Istria', *Austrian History Yearbook*, vol. 43, pp. 116–37 (2012). Applies 'national indifference'.

[58] I. Banac, *The National Question in Yugoslavia: Origins, History, Politics* (Ithaca, 1984).

[59] M. Bergholz, 'Sudden Nationhood: The Microdynamics of Intercommunal Relations in Bosnia–Herzegovina after World War II', *American Historical Review*, vol. 118, no. 3 (2013), pp. 679–707.

[60] I. Blumi, *Reinstating the Ottomans: Alternative Balkan Modernities, 1800–1912* (Basingstoke, 2011). Anti-nationalist. See also [68].

[61] J. Byford, 'The Collaborationist Administration and the Treatment of the Jews in Nazi-Occupied Serbia', in S. P. Ramet and O. Listhaug (eds), *Serbia and the Serbs in World War Two* (Basingstoke, 2011).

[62] A. Djilas, *The Contested Country: Yugoslav Unity and Communist Revolution 1919–1953* (Cambridge MA, 1991). See esp. for Communist Party.

[63] D. Djokić, *Elusive Compromise: A History of Interwar Yugoslavia* (London, 2007). On 1918–41 politics.

[64] D. Djokić, *Pašić and Trumbić: The Kingdom of Serbs, Croats and Slovenes* (London, 2010). On unification.

[65] V. Drapac, *Constructing Yugoslavia: A Transnational History* (Basingstoke, 2010).

[66] T. Dulić, 'Ethnic Violence in Occupied Yugoslavia: Mass Killing from Above and Below', in Ker-Lindsay and Djokić (eds), *New Perspectives*, cited in [81].

[67] T. Dulić, 'Mass Killing in the Independent State of Croatia, 1941–1945: A Case for Comparative Research', *Journal of Genocide Research*, vol. 8, no. 3 (2006), pp. 255–81.

[68] J. V. A. Fine, *When Ethnicity Did Not Matter in the Balkans: A Study of Identity in Pre-Nationalist Croatia, Dalmatia, and Slavonia in the Medieval and Early-Modern Periods* (Ann Arbor, 2006). See also [60].

[69] F. Friedman, *The Bosnian Muslims: Denial of a Nation* (Boulder, 1996). From Ottoman era to 1990s.

[70] I. Goldstein, *Croatia: A History* (London, 1999).

[71] E. Greble, *Sarajevo, 1941–1945: Muslims, Christians, and Jews in Hitler's Europe* (Ithaca, 2011). See also [56].

[72] E. Hajdarpašić, 'Out of the Ruins of the Ottoman Empire: Reflections on the Ottoman Legacy in South-Eastern Europe', *Middle Eastern Studies*, vol. 44, no. 5 (2008), pp. 715–34.

[73] R. M. Hayden and T. D. Walker, 'Intersecting Religioscapes and Antagonistic Tolerance: Trajectories of Competition and Sharing

of Religious Spaces in the Balkans', *Space and Polity*, vol. 17, no. 3 (2013), pp. 320–34.

[74] M. A. Hoare, *The History of Bosnia* (London, 2007). On continuity of Bosnia.

[75] M. A. Hoare, *The Bosnian Muslims in the Second World War: A History* (London, 2013). Also covers Communist state-building after 1943.

[76] M. A. Hoare, *Genocide and Resistance in Hitler's Bosnia: The Partisans and the Chetniks 1941–1943* (Oxford, 2006).

[77] J. Irvine, 'The Croatian Spring and the Dissolution of Yugoslavia', in Cohen and Dragović-Soso (eds), *State Collapse*, cited in [9].

[78] C. Jelavich and B. Jelavich, *The Establishment of the Balkan National States, 1804–1920* (Seattle, 1977). Classic work on 19th century.

[79] D. Jović, *Yugoslavia: A State that Withered Away* (West Lafayette, 2009). Focus on Communist ideology.

[80] P. M. Judson, *Guardians of the Nation: Activists on the Language Frontiers of Imperial Austria* (Cambridge MA, 2006). Rethinking of 19th-century nationalism.

[81] J. Ker-Lindsay and D. Djokić (eds), *New Perspectives on Yugoslavia: Key Issues and Controversies* (London, 2011). Collects new research on 20th century.

[82] A. Korb, 'Understanding Ustaša Violence', *Journal of Genocide Research*, vol. 12, no. 1–2 (2010), pp. 1–18.

[83] J. R. Lampe, 'The Two Yugoslavias as Economic Unions', in Djokić (ed.), *Yugoslavism*, cited in [12].

[84] I. Lovrenović, *Bosnia: A Cultural History*, trans. S. W. Bičanić (London, 2001).

[85] B. Magaš, *Croatia through History* (London, 2007).

[86] N. J. Miller, *Between Nation and State: Serbian Politics in Croatia before the First World War* (Pittsburgh, 1997). On Croat–Serb Coalition.

[87] P. Mojzes, *Balkan Genocides: Holocaust and Ethnic Cleansing in the Twentieth Century* (Lanham, 2011). Compares the 20th-century conflicts.

[88] K. Morrison, *Montenegro: A Modern History* (London, 2007).

[89] K. Morrison and E. Roberts, *The Sandžak: A History* (London, 2013).

[90] P. H. Patterson, *Bought and Sold: Living and Losing the Good Life in Socialist Yugoslavia* (Ithaca, 2011). Reinterpreting Yugoslav social history.

[91] S. K. Pavlowitch, *Hitler's New Disorder: The Second World War in Yugoslavia* (London, 2008).

[92] S. K. Pavlowitch, *The Improbable Survivor: Yugoslavia and its Problems, 1918–1988* (Columbus, 1988).

[93] S. K. Pavlowitch, *Serbia: The History Behind the Name* (London, 2002).

[94] E. Roberts, *Realm of the Black Mountain: A History of Montenegro* (London, 2007).

[95] D. Rusinow, 'Reopening of the "National Question" in the 1960s', in Cohen and Dragović-Soso (eds), *State Collapse*, cited in [9].

[96] D. Rusinow, *The Yugoslav Experiment, 1948–1974* (London, 1977).

[97] Đ. Stefanović, 'Seeing the Albanians through Serbian Eyes: The Inventors of the Tradition of Intolerance and Their Critics, 1804–1939', *European History Quarterly*, vol. 35, no. 3 (2005), pp. 465–92. On persecution of Albanians.

[98] P. F. Sugar, *Southeastern Europe under Ottoman Rule, 1354–1804* (Seattle, 1977).

[99] M. Tanner, *Croatia: A Nation Forged in War*, 3rd ed. (New Haven, 2010).

[100] J. Tomasevich, 'Yugoslavia during the Second World War', in W. S. Vucinich (ed.), *Contemporary Yugoslavia: Twenty Years of Socialist Experiment* (Berkeley, 1969).

[101] S. L. Woodward, 'The Long Intervention: Continuity in the Balkan Theatre', *Review of International Studies*, vol. 39, no. 5 (2013), pp. 1169–87.

[102] T. Zahra, 'Imagined Noncommunities: National Indifference as a Category of Analysis', *Slavic Review*, vol. 69, no. 1 (2010), pp. 93–119.

[103] Z. Zlatar, 'The Building of Yugoslavia: The Yugoslav Idea and the First Common State of the South Slavs', *Nationalities Papers*, vol. 25, no. 3 (1997), pp. 387–406.

[104] S. Zukin, *Beyond Marx and Tito: Theory and Practice in Yugoslav Socialism* (Cambridge, 1975).

The 1980s crisis

[105] J. B. Allcock, 'In Praise of Chauvinism: Rhetorics of Nationalism in Yugoslav Politics', *Third World Quarterly*, vol. 11, no. 4 (1989), pp. 208–22.

[106] J. B. Allcock, 'Rural–Urban Differences and the Break-Up of Yugoslavia', *Balkanologie*, vol. 6, no. 1–2 (2002), pp. 101–25.

[107] R. Archer, 'Social Inequalities and the Study of Yugoslavia's Dissolution', in Bieber et al. (eds), *Debating*, cited in [7].

[108] M. Bakić-Hayden and R. M. Hayden, 'Orientalist Variations on the Theme "Balkans": Symbolic Geography in Recent Yugoslav Cultural Politics', *Slavic Review*, vol. 51, no. 1 (1992), pp. 1–15.

[109] L. Boban, 'Jasenovac and the Manipulation of History', *East European Politics and Societies*, vol. 4, no. 3 (1990), pp. 580–92. Compare [116].

[110] W. Bracewell, 'Rape in Kosovo: Masculinity and Serbian Nationalism', *Nationalities Papers*, vol. 6, no. 4 (2000), pp. 563–90.

[111] A. H. Budding, 'Systematic Crisis and National Mobilization: The Case of the "Memorandum of the Serbian Academy"', *Harvard Ukrainian Studies*, vol. 22 (1998), pp. 49–69.

[112] B. Denich, 'Dismembering Yugoslavia: Nationalist Ideologies and the Symbolic Revival of Genocide', *American Ethnologist*, vol. 21, no. 2 (1994), pp. 367–90.

[113] D. Djokić, 'The Second World War II: Discourses of Reconciliation in Serbia and Croatia in the Late 1980s and Early 1990s', *Journal of Southern Europe and the Balkans*, vol. 4, no. 2 (2002), pp. 127–40.

[114] J. Dragović-Soso, *'Saviours of the Nation': Serbia's Intellectual Opposition and the Revival of Nationalism* (London, 2002). Also covers Slovenia.

[115] D. A. Dyker, *Yugoslavia: Socialism, Development and Debt* (London, 1990). Socio-economic focus.

[116] R. M. Hayden, 'Recounting the Dead: The Rediscovery and Redefinition of Wartime Massacres in Late- and Post-Communist Yugoslavia', in R. S. Watson (ed.), *Memory, History and Opposition Under State Socialism* (Santa Fe, 1994).

[117] B. Horvat, 'The Association for Yugoslav Democratic Initiative', in Djokić (ed.), *Yugoslavism*, cited in [12].

[118] B. Horvat, 'Two Widespread Ideological Deviations in Contemporary Yugoslav Society', *Eastern European Economics*, vol. 23, no. 1 (1984), pp. 45–57.

[119] M. Palairet, 'The Inter-Regional Struggle for Resources and the Fall of Yugoslavia', in Cohen and Dragović-Soso (eds), *State Collapse*, cited in [9].

[120] R. Petrović and M. Blagojević, *The Migration of Serbs and Montenegrins from Kosovo and Metohija: Results of the Survey Conducted in 1985–1986* (Belgrade, 1992).

[121] K. Verdery, *The Political Lives of Dead Bodies: Reburial and Postsocialist Change* (New York, 1999). Puts Yugoslavia in eastern European context.

[122] A. Wachtel and P. J. Marković, 'A Last Attempt at Educational Integration: The Failure of Common Educational Cores in Yugoslavia in the Early 1980s', in Cohen and Dragović-Soso (eds), *State Collapse*, cited in [9].

[123] S. L. Woodward, *Socialist Unemployment: The Political Economy of Yugoslavia 1945–1990* (Princeton, 1995).

Serbia under Milošević

[124] F. Bieber, 'Nationalist Mobilization and Stories of Serb Suffering: The Kosovo Myth from 600th Anniversary to the Present', *Rethinking History*, vol. 6, no. 1 (2002), pp. 95–110.

[125] S. Biserko, *Yugoslavia's Implosion: The Fatal Attraction of Serbian Nationalism* (Norwegian Helsinki Committee, 2012). By well-known Serbian human rights activist.

[126] A. H. Budding, 'From Dissidents to Presidents: Dobrica Ćosić and Vojislav Koštunica Compared', *Contemporary European History*, vol. 13, no. 2 (2004), pp. 185–201.

[127] D. Bujošević and I. Radovanović, *The Fall of Milošević: The October 5th Revolution* (Basingstoke, 2003).

[128] L. J. Cohen, *Serpent in the Bosom: The Rise and Fall of Slobodan Milošević*, rev. ed. (Boulder, 2002).

[129] P. J. Cohen, 'The Ideology and Historical Continuity of Serbia's Anti-Islamic Policy', *Islamic Studies*, vol. 36, no. 2–3 (1997), pp. 361–82.

[130] I. Čolović, *The Politics of Symbol in Serbia*, trans. C. Hawkesworth (London, 2002).

[131] C. Costamagna, 'Milošević Posing as Saviour of the Communist Regime: A Reassessment', in Bieber et al. (eds), *Debating*, cited in [7].

[132] O. Fridman, '"It Was Like Fighting a War with Our Own People": Anti-War Activism in Serbia During the 1990s', *Nationalities Papers*, vol. 39, no. 4 (2011), pp. 507–22.

[133] E. D. Gordy, *The Culture of Power in Serbia: Nationalism and the Destruction of Alternatives* (University Park, 1999). Also integrates popular music into politics.

[134] M. A. Hoare, 'Slobodan Milošević's Place in Serbian History', *European History Quarterly*, vol. 36, no. 3 (2006), pp. 445–62. Includes critique of [79].

[135] S. Jansen, 'Victims, Underdogs and Rebels: Discursive Practices of Resistance in Serbian Protest', *Critique of Anthropology*, vol. 20, no. 4 (2000), pp. 393–419.

[136] T. Judah, *The Serbs: History, Myth, and the Destruction of Yugoslavia*, 3rd ed. (New Haven, 2009).

[137] E. Kerenji, 'Vojvodina Since 1988', in Ramet and Pavlaković (eds), *Serbia Since 1989*, cited in [144].

[138] A. LeBor, *Milosevic: A Biography* (London, 2002).

[139] M. Miljković and M. A. Hoare, 'Crime and the Economy Under Milošević and His Successors', in Ramet and Pavlaković (eds), *Serbia Since 1989*, cited in [144].

[140] G. Musić, *Serbia's Working Class in Transition 1988–2013* (Belgrade, 2013).

[141] G. Musić, '"They Came as Workers and Returned as Serbs": The Role of Rakovica's Blue-Collar Workers in Serbian Social Mobilizations of the Late 1980s', in R. Archer et al. (eds), *Social Inequalities and Discontent in Yugoslavia* (Farnham, 2015).

[142] V. Pavlaković, 'Serbia Transformed? Political Dynamics in the Milošević Era and After', in Ramet and Pavlaković (eds), *Serbia Since 1989*, cited in [144].

[143] N. Popov (ed.), *The Road to War in Serbia: Trauma and Catharsis* (Budapest, 2000). Perspectives from Serbian independent media.

[144] S. P. Ramet and V. Pavlaković (eds) *Serbia since 1989: Politics and Society Under Milošević and After* (Seattle, 2005).

[145] B. Šušak, 'An Alternative to War', in Popov (ed.), *Road to War*, cited in [143].

[146] R. Thomas, *Serbia under Milošević: Politics in the 1990s* (London, 1999).

[147] M. Upchurch and D. Marinković, *Workers and Revolution in Serbia: From Tito to Milošević and Beyond* (Manchester, 2013). On workers' movement.

[148] N. Vladisavljević, *Serbia's Antibureaucratic Revolution: Milošević, the Fall of Communism and Nationalist Mobilization* (Basingstoke, 2008). New angle on 1980s public mobilization.

[149] M. Živković, *Serbian Dreambook: National Imaginary in the Time of Milošević* (Bloomington, 2011). Anthropology of culture.

The Slovenian and Croatian wars of independence

[150] N. Arielli, 'In Search of Meaning: Foreign Volunteers in the Croatian Armed Forces, 1991–95', *Contemporary European History*, vol. 21, no. 1 (2011), pp. 1–17.

[151] N. Barić, 'Before the Storm: Croatian Efforts to Integrate Republic of Serb Krajina from Early 1992 to August 1995', in Bieber et al. (eds), *Debating*, cited in [7]. By author of key work in Croatian on RSK.

[152] F. Bieber, 'The Role of the Yugoslav People's Army in the Disintegration of Yugoslavia: An Army without a State?', in Cohen and Dragović-Soso (eds), *State Collapse*, cited in [9].

[153] B. Bilić and V. Janković (eds), *Resisting the Evil: (Post-)Yugoslav Anti-War Contention* (Baden-Baden, 2012). On peace activism. See also [160].

[154] R. Brubaker, *Nationalism Reframed: Nationhood and the National Question in the New Europe* (Cambridge, 1996). Constructivist.

[155] M. J. Calic et al., 'Ethnic Cleansing and War Crimes, 1991–95', in Ingrao and Emmert (eds), *Confronting*, cited in [20]. Compare [163].

[156] C. Carmichael, *Ethnic Cleansing in the Balkans: Nationalism and the Destruction of Tradition* (London, 2002).

[157] N. Caspersen, 'Belgrade, Pale, Knin: Kin-State Control over Rebellious Puppets?', *Europe–Asia Studies*, vol. 59, no. 4 (2007), pp. 621–41.

[158] T. Cushman, 'Collective Punishment and Forgiveness: Judgments of Post-Communist National Identities by the "Civilized" West', in S. G. Meštrović (ed.), *Genocide After Emotion: The Postemotional Balkan War* (London, 1996).

[159] T. Cushman, *Critical Theory and the War in Bosnia and Croatia.* Donald W. Treadgold Papers in Russian, East European, and Central Asian Studies 13 (Seattle, 1997).

[160] A. Dević, 'Anti-War Initiatives and the Un-Making of Civic Identities in the Former Yugoslav Republics', *Journal of Historical Sociology*, vol. 10, no. 2 (1997), pp. 127–56. See also [153].

[161] T. Dulić and R. Kostić, 'Yugoslavs in Arms: Guerrilla Tradition, Total Defence and the Ethnic Security Dilemma', *Europe–Asia Studies*, vol. 62, no. 7 (2010), pp. 1051–72.

[162] J. Glaurdić, 'Inside the Serbian War Machine: The Milošević Telephone Intercepts, 1991–1992', *East European Politics and Societies*, vol. 23, no. 1 (2009), pp. 86–104.

[163] J. Glaurdić, 'Review Essay: Confronting the Yugoslav Controversies: A Scholars' Initiative', *East European Politics and Societies*, vol. 24, no. 2 (2010), pp. 294–309. Severe criticisms of 1st ed. of [20].

[164] E. D. Gordy, 'Destruction of the Yugoslav Federation: Policy or Confluence of Tactics?', in Cohen and Dragović-Soso (eds), *State Collapse*, cited in [9].

[165] J. Gow, *The Serbian Project and its Adversaries: A Strategy of War Crimes* (London, 2003). Developed from advice to ICTY prosecutors.

[166] H. Grandits and C. Leutloff, 'Discourses, Actors, Violence: The Organisation of War-Escalation in the Krajina Region of Croatia 1990–91', in J. Koehler and C. Zürcher (eds), *Potentials of Disorder* (Manchester, 2003).

[167] M. Hadžić, 'The Army's Use of Trauma', in Popov (ed.), *Road to War*, cited in [143].

[168] P. Hockenos, *Homeland Calling: Exile Patriotism and the Balkan Wars* (Ithaca, 2003). On diaspora nationalism.

[169] J. Horncastle, 'Reaping the Whirlwind: Total National Defense's Role in Slovenia's Bid for Secession', *Journal of Slavic Military Studies*, vol. 26, no. 3 (2013), pp. 528–50.

[170] M. Ignatieff, *Blood and Belonging: Journeys into the New Nationalism* (London, 1993). On nationalism in world politics.

[171] D. Jović, 'The Slovenian–Croatian Confederal Proposal: A Tactical Move or an Ultimate Solution?', in Cohen and Dragović-Soso (eds), *State Collapse*, cited in [9].

[172] R. Kaplan, *Balkan Ghosts: A Journey through History* (New York, 1993). Travel writing with one chapter on Croatia.

[173] P. Kolstø and D. Pauković, 'The Short and Brutish Life of Republika Srpska Krajina: Failure of a De Facto State', *Ethnopolitics*, vol. 13, no. 4 (2014), pp. 309–27.

[174] C. S. Lilly and J. A. Irvine, 'Negotiating Interests: Women and Nationalism in Serbia and Croatia, 1990–1997', *East European Politics and Societies*, vol. 16, no. 1 (2002), pp. 109–44.

[175] T. Mastnak, 'The Slovene Story', *Praxis International*, vol. 4 (1993), pp. 373–88. On civil society.

[176] M. Milivojević, 'The Armed Forces of Yugoslavia: Sliding into War', in Ramet and Adamovich (eds), *Beyond Yugoslavia*, cited in [31].

[177] R. Mills, 'Fighters, Footballers and Nation Builders: Wartime Football in the Serb-Held Territories of the Former Yugoslavia, 1991–1996', *Sport in Society*, vol. 16, no. 8 (2013), pp. 945–72.

[178] J. Mostov, 'Sexing the Nation/Desexing the Body: Politics of National Identity in the Former Yugoslavia', in T. Mayer (ed.), *Gender Ironies of Nationalism: Sexing the Nation* (London, 2000).

[179] V. Pavlaković, 'Symbols and the Culture of Memory in Republika Srpska Krajina', *Nationalities Papers*, vol. 41, no. 6 (2013), pp. 893–909.

[180] J. J. Sadkovich, 'Patriots, Villains, and Franjo Tuđman', *Review of Croatian History*, vol. 2 (2006), pp. 247–80. Defends Tuđman.

[181] L. Spaskovska, 'Landscapes of Resistance, Hope and Loss: Yugoslav Supra-Nationalism and Anti-Nationalism', in Bilić and Janković (eds), *Resisting the Evil*, cited in [153].

[182] M. Špegelj, 'The First Phase, 1990–1992: The JNA Prepares for Aggression and Croatia for Defence', in Magaš and Žanić (eds), *The War in Croatia and Bosnia-Herzegovina, 1991–1995*, cited in [25]. By first Croatian defence minister.

[183] F. Strazzari, 'The Decade Horribilis: Organized Violence and Organized Crime along the Balkan Peripheries, 1991–2001', *Mediterranean Politics*, vol. 12, no. 2 (2007), pp. 185–209.

[184] A. Tus, 'The War in Slovenia and Croatia up to the Sarajevo Ceasefire', in Magaš and Žanić (eds), *The War in Croatia and Bosnia-Herzegovina, 1991–1995,*, cited in [25]. By Croatian Army chief of staff at time.

[185] O. Žunec, 'Operations Flash and Storm', in Magaš and Žanić (eds), *The War in Croatia and Bosnia-Herzegovina, 1991–1995*, cited in [25].

Post-independence Slovenia and Croatia

[186] J. Ashbrook, 'Politicization of Identity in a European Borderland: Istria, Croatia, and Authenticity, 1990–2003', *Nationalities Papers*, vol. 39, no. 6 (2011), pp. 871–97. On Istrian challenge to Tuđman.

[187] C. Baker, *Sounds of the Borderland: Popular Music, War and Nationalism in Croatia since 1991* (Farnham, 2010).

[188] A. J. Bellamy, *The Formation of Croatian National Identity: A Centuries-Old Dream?* (Manchester, 2003). On contestedness of national identity narratives.

[189] J. Benderly and E. Kraft (eds), *Independent Slovenia: Origins, Movements, Prospects* (New York, 1994).

[190] M. Billig, *Banal Nationalism* (London, 1995). Some discussion of Croatia.

[191] D. Brentin, '"A Lofty Battle for the Nation": The Social Roles of Sport in Tudjman's Croatia', *Sport in Society*, vol. 16, no. 8 (2013), pp. 993–1008.

[192] J. Dedić et al., *The Erased: Organized Innocence and the Politics of Exclusion* (Ljubljana, 2003). Critiques consequences of Slovenian citizenship laws.

[193] D. Fink-Hafner, 'Slovenia Since 1989', in Ramet (ed.), *Central and Southeast European Politics since 1989*, cited in [30].

[194] J. Gow and C. Carmichael, *Slovenia and the Slovenes: A Small State and the New Europe* (London, 2000).

[195] L. Hansen, 'Slovenian Identity: State-Building on the Balkan Border', *Alternatives: Global, Local, Political*, vol. 21, no. 4 (1996), pp. 473–95.

[196] R. Iveković, 'The New Democracy: With Women or without Them?', in Ramet and Adamovich (eds), *Beyond Yugoslavia*, cited in [31].

[197] V. Jalušič, 'Troubles with Democracy: Women and Slovene Independence', in Benderly and Kraft (eds), *Independent Slovenia*, cited in [189].

[198] T. Radanović Felberg and L. Šarić, 'Discursive Construction of Language Identity through Disputes in Croatian and Montenegrin Media', *Scando-Slavica*, vol. 59, no. 1 (2013), pp. 7–31.

[199] M. Razsa and N. Lindstrom, 'Balkan is Beautiful: Balkanism in the Political Discourse of Tuđman's Croatia', *East European Politics and Societies*, vol. 18, no. 4 (2004), pp. 628–50.

[200] D. Ugrešić, *The Culture of Lies: Antipolitical Essays*, trans. C. Hawkesworth (London, 1998). Anti-nationalist.

[201] G. Uzelak [Uzelac], 'Franjo Tudjman's Nationalist Ideology', *East European Quarterly*, vol. 31, no. 4 (1998), pp. 449–72. Discourse analysis.

[202] Z. Volcic, '"The Machine that Creates Slovenians": The Role of Slovenian Public Broadcasting in Re-Affirming and Re-Inventing the Slovenian National Identity', *National Identities*, vol. 7, no. 3 (2005), pp. 287–308.

Bosnia-Herzegovina

[203] N. Andjelić, *Bosnia-Herzegovina: The End of a Legacy* (London, 2003). Short-term background.

[204] P. Andreas, *Blue Helmets and Black Markets: The Business of Survival in the Siege of Sarajevo* (Ithaca, 2007). Covers UN and also organized crime.

[205] I. Armakolas, Ioannis. 'The "Paradox" of Tuzla City: Explaining Non-Nationalist Local Politics during the Bosnian War', *Europe–Asia Studies*, vol. 63, no. 2 (2011), pp. 229–61.

[206] E. Bećirević, *Genocide on the Drina River* (New Haven, 2014). 'Maximalist' approach to defining genocide against Bosniaks.

[207] E. Bećirević, 'The Issue of Genocidal Intent and Denial of Genocide: A Case Study of Bosnia and Herzegovina', *East European Politics and Societies*, vol. 24, no. 4 (2010), pp. 480–502. See also [368].

[208] M. Bell, *In Harm's Way: Bosnia: A War Reporter's Story*, 3rd ed. (London, 2012). Memoir.

[209] B. Bogdanović, 'The City and Death', trans. M. H. Heim, in J. Labon (ed.), *Balkan Blues: Writing out of Yugoslavia* (Evanston, 1995). Rural-vs.-urban interpretation.

[210] X. Bougarel, 'Yugoslav Wars: The "Revenge of the Countryside" Between Sociological Reality and Nationalist Myth', *East European Quarterly*, vol. 33, no. 2 (1999), pp. 157–75.

[211] X. Bougarel, 'Bosnian Muslims and the Yugoslav Idea', in Djokić (ed.), *Yugoslavism*, cited in [12].

[212] T. Bringa, *Being a Muslim the Bosnian Way: Identity and Community in a Central Bosnian Village* (Princeton, 1995). Focus on pre-war.

[213] S. L. Burg and P. Shoup, *The War in Bosnia-Herzegovina: Ethnic Conflict and International Intervention* (London, 1999). Focus on military/political institutions.

[214] D. Campbell, 'Atrocity, Memory, Photography: Imaging the Concentration Camps of Bosnia – The Case of ITN Versus Living Marxism, Part 1', *Journal of Human Rights*, vol. 1, no. 1 (2002), pp. 1–33.

[215] D. Campbell, *National Deconstruction: Violence, Identity, and Justice in Bosnia* (Minneapolis, 1998). Deconstructionist.

[216] N. Cigar, *Genocide in Bosnia: The Policy of 'Ethnic Cleansing'* (College Station, 1995).

[217] N. Cigar and P. Williams, *Indictment at The Hague: The Milošević Regime and Crimes of the Balkan Wars* (New York, 2002).

[218] M. Coward, 'Urbicide in Bosnia', in S. Graham (ed.), *Cities, War and Terrorism: Towards an Urban Geopolitics* (Oxford, 2004).

[219] J. Crampton, 'Bordering on Bosnia', *GeoJournal*, vol. 39, no. 4 (1996), pp. 353–61. Critiques ethnicity/territory nexus.

[220] J. Divjak, 'The First Phase, 1992–1993: Struggle for Survival and Genesis of the Army of Bosnia-Herzegovina', in Magaš and Žanić (eds), *The War in Croatia and Bosnia-Herzegovina, 1991–1995*, cited in [25]. By a senior ARBiH general 1992–94.

[221] R. J. Donia, *Radovan Karadžić: Architect of the Bosnian Genocide* (Cambridge, 2014). Currently most detailed work on wartime RS.

[222] R. J. Donia, *Sarajevo: A Biography* (London, 2006).

[223] R. J. Donia and J. V. A. Fine, *Bosnia and Hercegovina: A Tradition Betrayed* (New York, 1994). Defence of Bosnian multi-ethnicity. See also [240].

[224] A. Galijaš, 'What Do We Know About the *Lebenswelt* of Yugoslavs?', in Bieber et al. (eds), *Debating*, cited in [7]. On Banja Luka.

[225] J. Gow et al. (eds), *Bosnia by Television* (London, 1996). Comparative study of news.

[226] H. Griffiths, 'A Political Economy of Ethnic Conflict: Ethno-Nationalism and Organised Crime', *Civil Wars*, vol. 2, no. 2 (1999), pp. 56–73.

[227] R. Gutman, *A Witness to Genocide: The First Inside Account of the Horrors of 'Ethnic Cleansing' in Bosnia* (Shaftesbury, 1993). See also [254].

[228] H. Halilovich, *Places of Pain: Forced Displacement, Popular Memory and Trans-Local Identities in Bosnian War-Torn Communities* (Oxford, 2013).

[229] M. A. Hoare, 'The Bosnian War's Forgotten Turning Point: The Bihać Crisis of Autumn 1994', *Journal of Slavic Military Studies*, vol. 24, no. 1 (2011), pp. 88–114.

[230] M. A. Hoare, *How Bosnia Armed* (London, 2004). Short-term military background.

[231] J. W. Honig and N. Both, *Srebrenica: Record of a War Crime* (London, 1996).

[232] J. Hyndman, 'Preventative, Palliative, or Punitive? Safe Spaces in Bosnia-Herzegovina, Somalia, and Sri Lanka', *Journal of Refugee Studies*, vol. 16, no. 2 (2003), pp. 167–85.

[233] C. Ingrao et al., 'Safe Areas', in 2nd ed. of Ingrao and Emmert, *Confronting*, cited in [20].

[234] V. Janković, 'International Peace Activists in the Former Yugoslavia', in Bilić and Janković (eds), *Resisting the Evil*, cited in [153].

[235] H. Karčić, '"Fear Not, For You Have Brothers in Greece": A Research Note', *Genocide Studies and Prevention*, vol. 3, no. 1 (2008), pp. 147–52. On Greek volunteers.

[236] V. Kesić, 'A Response to Catharine MacKinnon's Article "Turning Rape into Pornography: Postmodern Genocide"', *Hastings Women's Law Journal*, vol. 5 (1994), pp. 267–80. Compare vs. [239].

[237] L. Kurtović, 'The Paradoxes of Wartime "Freedom": Alternative Culture during the Siege of Sarajevo', in Bilić and Janković (eds), *Resisting the Evil*, cited in [153].

[238] I. Maček, *Sarajevo under Siege: Anthropology in Wartime* (Philadelphia, 2009). Ethnography.

[239] C. MacKinnon, 'Crimes of War, Crimes of Peace', *UCLA Women's Law Journal*, vol. 4 (1993), pp. 59–86. Compare vs. [236].

[240] R. Mahmutćehajić, *The Denial of Bosnia* (University Park, 2000). See also [223].

[241] N. Malcolm, *Bosnia: A Short History*, updated ed. (London, 1996).

[242] R. Mills, 'Velež Mostar Football Club and the Demise of "Brotherhood and Unity" in Yugoslavia, 1922–2009', *Europe–Asia Studies*, vol. 62, no.7 (2010), pp. 1107–33.

[243] J. Mujanović, 'Princip, Valter, Pejić and the Raja: Elite Domination and Betrayal in Bosnia-Herzegovina', *South-East European Journal of Political Science*, vol. 1, no. 3 (2013), pp. 106–20.

[244] J. Mustapha, 'The Mujahideen in Bosnia: The Foreign Fighter as Cosmopolitan Citizen and/or Terrorist', *Citizenship Studies*, vol. 17, no. 6–7 (2013), pp. 742–55.

[245] L. J. Nettelfield, 'Research and Repercussions of Death Tolls: The Case of the Bosnian Book of the Dead', in P. Andreas and K. M. Greenhill (eds), *Sex, Drugs and Body Counts: The Politics of Numbers in Global Crime and Conflict* (Ithaca, 2010).

[246] C. A. Nielsen, 'Surmounting the Myopic Focus on Genocide: The Case of the War in Bosnia and Herzegovina', *Journal of Genocide Research*, vol. 15, no. 1 (2013), pp. 21–39. On limitations of debate over genocide recognition.

[247] D. Rohde, *Endgame: The Betrayal and Fall of Srebrenica, Europe's Worst Massacre since World War II*, 2nd ed. (New York, 2012).

[248] M. Sells, *The Bridge Betrayed: Religion and Genocide in Bosnia* (Berkeley, 1996).

[249] C. R. Shrader, *The Muslim – Croat Civil War in Central Bosnia: A History* (College Station, 2004). Attempts to hold ARBiH responsible.

[250] A. Stiglmayer (ed.), *Mass Rape: The War against Women in Bosnia-Herzegovina* (Lincoln, 1994). See also [239].

[251] E. Tabeau and J. Bijak, 'War-Related Deaths in the 1992–1995 Armed Conflicts in Bosnia and Herzegovina: A Critique of Previous Estimates and Recent Results', *European Journal of Population*, vol. 21, no. 2–3 (2005), pp. 187–215. ICTY figures.

[252] G. Toal and C. T. Dahlman, *Bosnia Remade: Ethnic Cleansing and its Reversal* (Oxford, 2011). Deconstructs ethno-territorial assumptions.

[253] M. Velikonja, *Religious Separation and Political Intolerance in Bosnia-Herzegovina*, trans. R. Ng'inja (College Station, 2003).

[254] E. Vulliamy, *Seasons in Hell: Understanding Bosnia's War* (London, 1994). See also [227].

[255] I. Wesselingh and A. Vaulerin, *Raw Memory: Prijedor, Laboratory of Ethnic Cleansing*, trans. J. Howe (London, 2005).

[256] H. Yamashita, *Humanitarian Space and International Politics: The Creation of Safe Areas* (Aldershot, 2004).

Diplomatic aspects

[257] M. Banks and M. Wolfe Murray, 'Ethnicity and Reports of the 1992–95 Bosnian Conflict', in T. Allen and J. Seaton (eds), *The Media of Conflict: War Reporting and Representations of Ethnic Violence* (London, 1999). Critiques Western media representation of ethnicity.

[258] D. Campbell, 'Apartheid Cartography: The Political Anthropology and Spatial Effects of International Diplomacy in Bosnia', *Political Geography*, vol. 18, no. 4 (1999), pp. 395–435. See also [252].

[259] D. Conversi, 'German-Bashing and the Breakup of Yugoslavia', Donald W. Treadgold Papers in Russian, East European, and Central Asian Studies 16 (Seattle, 1998). Compare vs. [260].

[260] B. Crawford, 'Explaining Defection from International Cooperation: Germany's Unilateral Recognition of Croatia', *World Politics*, vol. 48, no. 4 (1996), pp. 482–521. Compare vs. [259].

[261] D. N. Gibbs, *First Do No Harm: Humanitarian Intervention and the Destruction of Yugoslavia* (Nashville, 2009). Severely criticized by [45].

[262] J. Glaurdić, *The Hour of Europe: Western Powers and the Breakup of Yugoslavia* (New Haven, 2011). New archival diplomatic history.

[263] J. Gow, *Triumph of the Lack of Will: International Diplomacy and the Yugoslav War* (London, 1997).

[264] N. Gowing, 'Real-Time TV Coverage from War: Does It Make or Break Government Policy?', in Gow et al. (eds), *Bosnia by Television*, cited in [225].

[265] P. Hammond, *Framing Post Cold-War Conflicts: The Media and International Intervention* (Manchester, 2007). Accuses media of anti-Serb bias.

[266] L. Hansen, *Security as Practice: Discourse Analysis and the Bosnian War* (London, 2006). On 'Balkan violence' and 'genocide' discourses.

[267] G. Kent, *Framing War and Genocide: British Policy and News Media Reaction to the War in Bosnia* (Cresskill, 2006). Argues media relativized the war.

[268] S. Power, *A Problem from Hell: America and the Age of Genocide* (London, 2002). Defends intervention to prevent genocide.

[269] P. Radan, 'The Badinter Arbitration Commission and the Partition of Yugoslavia', *Nationalities Papers*, vol. 25, no. 3 (1997), pp. 537–57.

[270] B. Radeljić, *Europe and the Collapse of Yugoslavia: The Role of Non-State Actors and European Diplomacy* (London, 2012). On EC and Catholic Church.

[271] D. Rieff, *Slaughterhouse: Bosnia and the Failure of the West* (New York, 1996).

[272] B. Robison, 'Putting Bosnia in Its Place: Critical Geopolitics and the Representation of Bosnia in the British Print Media', *Geopolitics*, vol. 9, no. 2 (2004), pp. 378–401.

[273] B. Simms, *Unfinest Hour: Britain and the Destruction of Bosnia* (London, 2002).

[274] E. Vulliamy, 'Bosnia: The Crime of Appeasement', *International Affairs*, vol. 74, no. 1 (1998), pp. 73–91. By journalist who reported from Omarska.

Kosovo

[275] N. Chomsky, *The New Military Humanism: Lessons from Kosovo* (London, 1999). See also [265].

[276] E. A. Dauphinée, 'Rambouillet: A Critical (Re)Assessment', in F. Bieber and Z. Daskalovski (eds), *Understanding the War in Kosovo* (London, 2003).

[277] A. Di Lellio and S. Schwandner-Sievers, 'The Legendary Commander: The Construction of an Albanian Master-Narrative in Post-War Kosovo', *Nations and Nationalism*, vol. 12, no. 3 (2006), pp. 513–29. On memory of Jashari.

[278] E. Herring, 'From Rambouillet to the Kosovo Accords: NATO's War against Serbia and its Aftermath', *International Journal of Human Rights*, vol. 4, no. 3–4 (2000), pp. 224–45. Early overview.

[279] M. Ignatieff, *Virtual War: Kosovo and Beyond* (London, 2001).

[280] T. Judah, *Kosovo: War and Revenge*, 2nd ed. (New Haven, 2002).

[281] T. Keenan, 'Looking like Flames and Falling like Stars: Kosovo, "the First Internet War"', *Social Identities*, vol. 7, no. 4 (2001), pp. 539–50.

[282] J. Ker-Lindsay, *Kosovo: The Path to Contested Statehood in the Balkans* (London, 2009). On 1999–2008.

[283] M. Koskenniemi, '"The Lady Doth Protest Too Much": Kosovo and the Turn to Ethics in International Law', *Modern Law Review*, vol. 65, no. 2 (2002), pp. 159–75.

[284] D. Kostovicova, *Kosovo: The Politics of Identity and Space* (London, 2005).

[285] G. Krasniqi, 'Revisiting Nationalism in Yugoslavia: An Inside-Out View of the Nationalist Movement in Kosovo', in Bieber et al. (eds), *Debating*, cited in [7].

[286] N. Malcolm, *Kosovo: A Short History*, 2nd ed. (London, 1999).

[287] J. E. Mertus, *Kosovo: How Myths and Truths Started a War* (Berkeley, 1999). On 1980s.

[288] J. Pettifer, *The Kosova Liberation Army: Underground War to Balkan Insurgency, 1948–2001* (London, 2012).

[289] B. Pula, 'The Emergence of the Kosovo "Parallel State," 1988–1992', *Nationalities Papers*, vol. 32, no. 4 (2004), pp. 797–826.

[290] S. Schwandner-Sievers, 'Invisible – Inaudible: Albanian Memories of Socialism after the War in Kosovo', in M. Todorova and Z. Gille (eds), *Post-Communist Nostalgia* (Oxford, 2010).

[291] S. Schwandner-Sievers, 'The Bequest of *Ilegalja*: Contested Memories and Moralities in Contemporary Kosovo', *Nationalities Papers*, vol. 41, no. 6 (2013), pp. 953–70. On Albanian underground movement.

[292] D. Triantaphyllou, 'Kosovo Today: Is There No Way Out of the Deadlock?', *European Security*, vol. 5, no. 2 (1996), pp. 279–302.

[293] M. Vickers, *Between Serb and Albanian: A History of Kosovo* (London, 1998).

[294] M. Weller, 'The Rambouillet Conference on Kosovo', *International Affairs*, vol. 75, no. 2 (1999), pp. 211–51.

Macedonia

[295] A. J. Bellamy, 'The New Wolves at the Door: Conflict in Macedonia', *Civil Wars*, vol. 5, no. 1 (2002), pp. 117–44.

[296] K. Brown, *The Past in Question: Modern Macedonia and the Uncertainties of Nation* (Princeton, 2003). Compare [302].

[297] C. S. Chivvis, 'The Making of Macedonia', *Survival*, vol. 50, no. 2 (2008), pp. 141–62.

[298] L. M. Danforth, *The Macedonian Conflict: Ethnic Nationalism in a Transnational World* (Princeton, 1995).

[299] R. Dimova, 'Consuming Ethnicity: Loss, Commodities, and Space in Macedonia', *Slavic Review*, vol. 69, no. 4 (2010), pp. 859–81.

[300] R. Hislope, 'Between a Bad Peace and a Good War: Insights and Lessons from the Almost-War in Macedonia', *Ethnic and Racial Studies*, vol. 26, no. 1 (2003), pp. 129–51.

[301] V. P. Neofotistos, *The Risk of War: Everyday Sociality in the Republic of Macedonia* (Philadelphia, 2012). Anthropological.

[302] H. Poulton, *Who Are the Macedonians?*, 2nd ed. (London, 2000). Compare [296].

[303] L. Spaskovska, 'The Fractured "We" and the Ethno-National "I": The Macedonian Citizenship Framework', *Citizenship Studies*, vol. 16, no. 3–4 (2012), pp. 383–96. Assesses Ohrid Agreement.

Consequences

[304] D. Arsenijević (ed.), *Unbribable Bosnia and Herzegovina: The Fight for the Commons* (Baden-Baden, 2015). On popular protest.

[305] C. Baker, 'Prosperity without Security: The Precarity of Interpreters in Postsocialist, Postconflict Bosnia-Herzegovina', *Slavic Review*, vol. 71, no. 4 (2012), pp. 849–72. On peacekeeping and employment.

[306] R. Belloni and F. Strazzari, 'Corruption in Post-Conflict Bosnia-Herzegovina and Kosovo: A Deal among Friends', *Third World Quarterly*, vol. 35, no. 5 (2014), pp. 855–71.

[307] S. Bose, *Bosnia after Dayton: Nationalist Partition and International Intervention* (Oxford, 2002).

[308] X. Bougarel et al. (eds), *The New Bosnian Mosaic: Identities, Memories and Moral Claims in a Post-War Society* (Aldershot, 2007). Argues for ethnographic approach.

[309] R. Caplan, *International Governance of War-Torn Territories: Rule and Reconstruction* (Oxford, 2005).

[310] D. Chandler, *Bosnia: Faking Democracy after Dayton*, 2nd ed. (London, 2000).

[311] D. Chandler, *Empire in Denial: The Politics of State-Building* (London, 2006).

[312] J. N. Clark, 'Giving Peace a Chance: Croatia's Branitelji and the Imperative of Reintegration', *Europe–Asia Studies*, vol. 65, no. 10 (2013b), pp. 1931–53. On veterans.

[313] G. Duijzings, 'Commemorating Srebrenica: History and the Politics of Memory in Eastern Bosnia', in Bougarel et al. (eds), *The New Bosnian Mosaic*, cited in [308].

[314] M. Eastmond, 'Reconciliation, Reconstruction, and Everyday Life in War-Torn Societies', *Focaal*, vol. 57 (2010), pp. 3–16. On concepts of reconciliation.

[315] E. D. Gordy, *Guilt, Responsibility and Denial: The Past at Stake in Post-Milošević Serbia* (Philadelphia, 2013).

[316] J. Greenberg, *After the Revolution: Youth, Democracy, and the Politics of Disappointment in Serbia* (Stanford, 2014).

[317] E. Helms, 'The Gender of Coffee: Women and Reconciliation Initiatives in Post-War Bosnia and Herzegovina', *Focaal*, vol. 57 (2010), pp. 17–32.

[318] E. Helms, *Innocence and Victimhood: Gender, Nation, and Women's Activism in Postwar Bosnia–Herzegovina* (Madison, 2013).

[319] P. Higate and M. Henry, *Insecure Spaces: Peacekeeping, Power and Performance in Haiti, Kosovo and Liberia* (London, 2009).

[320] S. Horvat and I. Štiks (eds), *Welcome to the Desert of Post-Socialism: Radical Politics after Yugoslavia* (London, 2015). New left-wing critiques.

[321] A. Hromadžić, *Citizens of an Empty Nation: Youth and State-Making in Postwar Bosnia-Herzegovina* (Philadelphia, 2015).

[322] A. Hromadžić, 'Discourses of Trans-Ethnic Narod in Postwar Bosnia and Herzegovina', *Nationalities Papers*, vol. 41, no. 2 (2013), pp. 259–75. See also [349].

[323] C. Hughes and V. Pupavac, 'Framing Societies: International Pathologisation of Cambodia and the Post-Yugoslav States', *Third World Quarterly*, vol. 26, no. 6 (2005), pp. 873–89. Comparative argument about international intervention.

[324] S. Jansen, 'Cosmopolitan Openings and Closures in Post-Yugoslav Antinationalism', in M. Nowicka and M. Rovisco (eds), *Cosmopolitanism in Practice* (Aldershot, 2008).

[325] S. Jansen, 'If Reconciliation is the Answer, Are We Asking the Right Questions?', *Studies in Social Justice*, vol. 7, no. 2 (2013), pp. 229–43. See also [314].

[326] S. Jansen, 'The Privatisation of Home and Hope: Return, Reforms and the Foreign Intervention in Bosnia-Herzegovina', *Dialectical Anthropology*, vol. 30, no. 3–4 (2006), pp. 177–99.

[327] S. Jansen, '*Refuchess*: Locating Bosniac Repatriates After the War in Bosnia-Herzegovina', *Population, Space and Place*, vol. 17 (2011), pp. 140–52. On refugee return.

[328] S. Jansen, 'The Violence of Memories: Local Narratives of the Past After Ethnic Cleansing in Croatia', *Rethinking History*, vol. 6, no. 1 (2002), pp. 77–93.

[329] A. Jeffrey, *The Improvised State: Sovereignty, Performance and Agency in Dayton Bosnia* (Oxford, 2012).

[330] S. Kappler and O. Richmond, 'Peacebuilding and Culture in Bosnia and Herzegovina: Resistance or Emancipation?', *Security Dialogue*, vol. 42, no. 3 (2011), pp. 261–78.

[331] G. Knaus and F. Martin, 'Lessons from Bosnia and Herzegovina: Travails of the European Raj', *Journal of Democracy*, vol. 14, no. 3 (2003), pp. 60–74. Likens OHR to British imperial rule in India.

[332] R. Mac Ginty and O. P. Richmond, 'The Local Turn in Peace Building: A Critical Agenda for Peace', *Third World Quarterly*, vol. 34, no. 5 (2013), pp. 763–83.

[333] J. Mannergren Selimović, 'Making Peace, Making Memory: Peacebuilding and Politics of Remembrance at Memorials of Mass Atrocities', *Peacebuilding*, vol. 1, no. 3 (2013), pp. 334–48.

[334] F. Markowitz, *Sarajevo: A Bosnian Kaleidoscope* (Urbana, 2010). On post-war identities.

[335] M. Mikuš, '"State Pride": Politics of LGBT Rights and Democratisation in "European Serbia"', *East European Politics and Societies*, vol. 25, no. 4 (2011), pp. 835–51.

[336] A. Mujkić, 'We, the Citizens of Ethnopolis', *Constellations*, vol. 14, no. 1 (2007), pp. 112–28. Critiques Dayton.

[337] L. J. Nettelfield and S. E. Wagner, *Srebrenica in the Aftermath of Genocide* (Cambridge, 2014). On survivors and memory.

[338] C. A. Nielsen, 'Stronger than the State? Football Hooliganism, Political Extremism and the Gay Pride Parades in Serbia', *Sport in Society*, vol. 16, no. 8 (2013), pp. 1038–53.

[339] J. Obradović-Wochnik, *Ethnic Conflict and War Crimes in the Balkans: The Narratives of Denial in Post-Conflict Serbia* (London, 2013).

[340] R. Paris, 'Saving Liberal Peacebuilding', *Review of International Studies*, vol. 36, no. 2 (2010), pp. 337–65.

[341] M. Pugh, 'Postwar Political Economy in Bosnia and Herzegovina: The Spoils of Peace', *Global Governance*, vol. 8, no. 4 (2002), pp. 467–82.

[342] M. Pugh, 'Rubbing Salt into War Wounds: Shadow Economies and Peacebuilding in Bosnia and Kosovo', *Problems of Post-Communism*, vol. 51, no. 3 (2004), pp. 53–60.

[343] J. Sardelić, 'Antiziganism as Cultural Racism: Before and After the Disintegration of Yugoslavia', in T. Agarin (ed.), *When Stereotype Meets Prejudice: Antiziganism in European Societies* (Stuttgart, 2014). On prejudice against Roma.

[344] M. Schäuble, *Narrating Victimhood: Gender, Religion and the Making of Place in Post-War Croatia* (Oxford, 2014). On Dalmatian hinterland.

[345] C. Sorabji, 'Managing Memories in Post-War Sarajevo: Individuals, Bad Memories, and New Wars', *Journal of the Royal Anthropological Institute*, vol. 12, no. 1 (2006), pp. 1–18.

[346] A. H. Stefansson, 'Homes in the Making: Property Restitution, Refugee Return, and Senses of Belonging in a Post-war Bosnian Town', *International Migration*, vol. 44, no. 3 (2006), pp. 115–39.

[347] A. H. Stefansson, 'Urban Exile: Locals, Newcomers and the Cultural Transformation of Sarajevo', in Bougarel et al. (eds), *The New Bosnian Mosaic*, cited in [308].

[348] G. Toal, '"Republika Srpska Will Have a Referendum": The Rhetorical Politics of Milorad Dodik', *Nationalities Papers*, vol. 41, no. 1 (2013), 166–204.

[349] H. Touquet, 'Multi-Ethnic Parties in Bosnia-Herzegovina: Naša Stranka and the Paradoxes of Postethnic Politics', *Studies in Ethnicity and Nationalism*, vol. 11, no. 3 (2011), pp. 451–67. See also [322].

[350] G. Visoka, 'The "Kafkaesque Accountability" of International Governance in Kosovo', *Journal of Intervention and Statebuilding*, vol. 6, no. 2 (2012), pp. 189–212.

[351] D. Zaum, 'Post-Conflict Statebuilding and Forced Migration', in A. Betts and G. Loescher (eds), *Refugees in International Relations* (Oxford, 2011).

War crimes trials

[352] J. B. Allcock et al., 'The International Criminal Tribunal for the Former Yugoslavia', in Ingrao and Emmert (eds), *Confronting*, cited in [20].

[353] T. Banjeglav, 'Dealing with the Past in Post-War Croatia: Perceptions, Problems, and Perspectives', in Simić and Volčič (eds), *Transitional Justice*, cited in [378].

[354] F. Bieber, 'Do Historians Need a Verdict?', in Waters (ed.), *Trial,* cited in [387].

[355] D. Buss, 'Prosecuting Mass Rape: *Prosecutor v. Dragoljub Kunarac, Radomir Kovac and Zoran Vukovic*', *Feminist Legal Studies,* vol. 10 (2002), pp. 91–9.

[356] J. N. Clark, 'Courting Controversy: The ICTY's Acquittal of Croatian Generals Gotovina and Markač', *Journal of International Criminal Justice,* vol. 11, no. 2 (2013), pp. 399–423.

[357] J. N. Clark, 'The "Crime of Crimes": Genocide, Criminal Trials and Reconciliation', *Journal of Genocide Research,* vol. 14, no. 1 (2012), pp. 55–77.

[358] J. N. Clark, 'Reconciliation through Remembrance? War Memorials and the Victims of Vukovar', *International Journal of Transitional Justice,* vol. 7, no. 1 (2012), pp. 116–35.

[359] R. J. Donia, 'History and the Court: The Role of History at the ICTY', *Prilozi,* vol. 41 (Sarajevo, 2012), pp. 13–20.

[360] S. Drakulić, *They Would Never Hurt a Fly: War Criminals on Trial in The Hague* (London, 2004).

[361] E. Elias-Bursać, *Translating Evidence and Interpreting Testimony at a War Crimes Tribunal: Working in a Tug-of-War* (London, 2015).

[362] J. Gow et al. (eds), *Prosecuting War Crimes: Lessons and Legacies of the International Criminal Tribunal for the Former Yugoslavia* (London, 2014).

[363] J. Gow and M. Michalski, 'Prosecuting with Pictures: Two Decades of Experience and Evolution', in Gow et al. (eds), *Prosecuting,* cited in [362].

[364] J. Hagan, *Justice in the Balkans: Prosecuting War Crimes in the Hague Tribunal* (Chicago, 2003).

[365] H. K. Haug, 'Debating the End of Yugoslavia in Post-Milošević Serbia', in Bieber et al. (eds), *Debating,* cited in [7]. On Koštunica's TRC.

[366] R. M. Hayden, 'Bosnia's Internal War and the International Criminal Tribunal', *Fletcher Forum of World Affairs,* vol. 22, no. 1 (1998), pp. 45–64. Argues ICTY mischaracterized Bosnian war.

[367] M. A. Hoare, 'Bosnia-Hercegovina and International Justice: Past Failures and Future Solutions', *East European Politics and Societies,* vol. 24, no. 2 (2010), pp. 191–205.

[368] M. A. Hoare, 'A Case Study in Underachievement: The International Courts and Genocide in Bosnia-Herzegovina', *Genocide Studies and Prevention,* vol. 6, no. 1 (2011), pp. 81–97. Argues ICTY not proactive enough.

[369] M. A. Hoare, 'Genocide in the Former Yugoslavia before and After Communism', *Europe–Asia Studies,* vol. 62, no. 7 (2010), pp. 1193–214.

[370] R. Hodžić, 'Living the Legacy of Mass Atrocities: Victims' Perspectives on War Crimes Trials', *Journal of International Criminal Justice,* vol. 8, no. 1 (2010), pp. 113–36. See also [379].

[371] R. Kerr, *The International Criminal Tribunal for the Former Yugoslavia: An Exercise in Law, Politics and Diplomacy* (Oxford, 2004).

[372] J. Mannergren Selimović, 'Perpetrators and Victims: Local Responses to the International Criminal Tribunal for the Former Yugoslavia', *Focaal*, vol. 57 (2010), pp. 50–61.

[373] C. A. Nielsen, 'Can We Salvage a History of the Former Yugoslav Conflicts from the Milošević Trial?', in Waters (ed.), *Trial*, cited in [387].

[374] V. Pavlaković, 'Better the Grave than a Slave: Croatia and the International Criminal Tribunal for the Former Yugoslavia', in S. P. Ramet et al., *Croatia since Independence: War, Politics, Society, Foreign Relations* (Munich, 2008).

[375] V. Petrović, 'A Crack in the Wall of Denial: The *Scorpions* Video In and Out of the Courtroom', in D. Žarkov and M. Glasius (eds), *Narratives of Justice In and Out of the Courtroom: Former Yugoslavia and Beyond* (New York, 2014).

[376] V. Petrović, 'Serbian Political Elites and the Vance – Owen Peace Plan: ICTY Documents as Historical Sources', in Bieber et al. (eds), *Debating*, cited in [7].

[377] W. A. Schabas, *The UN International Criminal Tribunals: The Former Yugoslavia, Rwanda and Sierra Leone* (Cambridge, 2006). Detailed comparative study.

[378] O. Simić and Z. Volčič (eds), *Transitional Justice and Civil Society in the Balkans* (New York, 2013).

[379] E. Stover, *The Witnesses: War Crimes and the Promise of Justice in The Hague* (Philadelphia, 2005). On survivor–witnesses' experiences.

[380] H. Subašić and N. Ćurak, 'History, the ICTY's Record, and the Bosnian Serb Culture of Denial', in Gow et al. (eds), *Prosecuting*, cited in [362].

[381] J. Subotić, *Hijacked Justice: Dealing with the Past in the Balkans* (Ithaca, 2009). Compares post-Yugoslav states.

[382] J. Subotić, 'Legitimacy, Scope, and Conflicting Claims on the ICTY: In the Aftermath of *Gotovina, Haradinaj* and *Perišić*', *Journal of Human Rights*, vol. 13, no. 2 (2014), pp. 170–85.

[383] F. Trix, 'Underwhelmed: Kosovar Albanians' Reactions to the Milošević Trial', in Waters (ed.), *Trial*, cited in [387].

[384] I. Vukušić, 'Judging Their Hero: Perceptions of the International Criminal Tribunal for the Former Yugoslavia in Croatia', in Gow et al. (eds), *Prosecuting*, cited in [362]. On Gotovina.

[385] T. W. Waters, 'The Forum: The International Criminal Tribunal for the Former Yugoslavia', in Waters (ed.), *Trial*, cited in [387].

[386] T. W. Waters, 'The Trial: IT–02–54, *Prosecutor v. Milošević*', in Waters (ed.), *Trial*, cited in [387].

[387] T. W. Waters (ed.), *The Milošević Trial: An Autopsy* (Oxford, 2014).

[388] R. A. Wilson, *Writing History in International Criminal Trials* (Cambridge, 2011). Deconstructs ICTY's production of evidence.

Culture and language

[389] R. Alexander, *Bosnian, Croatian, Serbian: A Grammar with Sociolinguistic Commentary* (Madison, 2006).

[390] R. Archer, 'Assessing Turbofolk Controversies: Popular Music between the Nation and the Balkans', *Southeastern Europe*, vol. 36 (2012), pp. 178–207. Reinterprets earlier approaches.

[391] M. Bakić-Hayden, 'Nesting Orientalisms: The Case of Former Yugoslavia', *Slavic Review*, vol. 54, no. 4 (1995), pp. 917–31.

[392] D. A. Buchanan (ed.), *Balkan Popular Culture and the Ottoman Ecumene: Music, Image, and Regional Political Discourse* (Lanham, 2007). Transnational.

[393] R. Bugarski, 'Language, Identity and Borders in the Former Serbo-Croatian Area', *Journal of Multilingual and Multicultural Development*, vol. 33, no. 3 (2012), pp. 219–35.

[394] R. Bugarski, 'What Happened to Serbo-Croatian?', in Gorup (ed.), *After Yugoslavia*, cited in [396].

[395] V. Goldsworthy, *Inventing Ruritania: The Imperialism of the Imagination*, updated ed. (New York, 2013). On fictional representations.

[396] R. Gorup (ed.), *After Yugoslavia: The Cultural Spaces of a Vanished Land* (Stanford, 2013).

[397] R. D. Greenberg, *Language and Identity in the Balkans* (Oxford, 2004). Compares post-Yugoslav states.

[398] A. Horton, 'The Vibrant Cinemas in the Post-Yugoslav Space', in Gorup (ed.), *After Yugoslavia*, cited in [396].

[399] D. Iordanova, *Cinema of Flames: Balkan Film, Culture and the Media* (London, 2001). On 'self-exoticism'.

[400] T. Judah, 'Yugoslavia is Dead: Long Live the Yugosphere', LSEE Research on South Eastern Europe Working Paper 1 (London, 2009).

[401] A. Kiossev, 'The Dark Intimacy: Maps, Identities, Acts of Identifications', in D. I. Bjelić and O. Savić (eds), *Balkan as Metaphor* (Cambridge MA, 2002). On cultural reclaiming of Balkans.

[402] G. Krasniqi, 'Socialism, National Utopia, and Rock Music: Inside the Albanian Rock Scene of Yugoslavia, 1970–1989', *East Central Europe*, vol. 38, no. 2 (2011), pp. 336–54.

[403] I. Kronja, 'Turbo Folk and Dance Music in 1990s Serbia: Media, Ideology and the Production of Spectacle', *Anthropology of East Europe Review*, vol. 22, no. 1 (2004), pp. 103–14. Feminist critique.

[404] M. Laušević, 'Some Aspects of Music and Politics in Bosnia', in J. M. Halpern and D. A. Kideckel (eds), *Neighbors at War: Anthropological Perspectives on Yugoslav Ethnicity, Culture and History* (University Park, 2000). On music as symbol of ethnicity.

[405] T. Z. Longinović, *Vampire Nation: Violence as Cultural Imaginary* (Durham NC, 2011). On representations of Serbs.

[406] T. Z. Longinović, 'Post-Yugoslav Emergence and the Creation of Difference', in Gorup (ed.), *After Yugoslavia*, cited in [396].

[407] D. Mišina, *Shake, Rattle and Roll: Yugoslav Rock Music and the Poetics of Social Critique* (Farnham, 2013). On 1980s.

[408] J. Mujanović, 'Hip-Hop as Critical Social Theory in Post-Dayton Bosnia-Herzegovina', in A. Helbig and M. Miszczynski (eds), *Hip-Hop in the East of Europe* (Bloomington, 2015).

[409] R. Okey, 'Serbian, Croatian, Bosnian?: Language and Nationality in the Lands of Former Yugoslavia', *East European Quarterly*, vol. 38, no. 4 (2004), pp. 419–41.

[410] J. Pavičić, 'From a Cinema of Hatred to a Cinema of Consciousness: Croatian Film after Yugoslavia', in A. Vidan and G. P. Crnković (eds), *In Contrast: Croatian Film Today* (Zagreb, 2012).

[411] S. Pettan (ed.), *Music, Politics and War: Views from Croatia* (Zagreb, 1998). Anthropology/ethnomusicology.

[412] A. Pisac, 'An Anthropology of Literary Success: "Hits", "Near-Misses" and "Failures" from Ex-Yugoslavia', *Wasafiri*, vol. 29, no. 2 (2014), pp. 58–64. Politics of translation.

[413] M. Pogačar, 'Punk Rock, the Alternative, and Political Appropriations', in O. Luthar (ed.), *The Land Between: A History of Slovenia*, 2nd ed. (Frankfurt, 2013).

[414] V. Pupavac, *Language Rights: From Free Speech to Linguistic Governance* (Basingstoke, 2012).

[415] L. V. Rasmussen, *Newly-Composed Folk Music of Yugoslavia* (London, 2002).

[416] J. Samson, *Music in the Balkans* (Leiden, 2013). Longue-durée approach.

[417] C. Silverman, *Romani Routes: Cultural Politics and Balkan Music in Diaspora* (Oxford, 2012).

[418] D. Škiljan, 'From Croato-Serbian to Croatian: Croatian Linguistic Identity', *Multilingua*, vol. 19, no. 1–2 (2000), pp. 3–20. Criticizes 1990s language policy.

[419] M. Todorova, *Imagining the Balkans*, updated ed. (Oxford, 2009).

[420] M. Velikonja, *Titostalgia: A Study of Nostalgia for Josip Broz* (Ljubljana, 2008).

[421] Z. Volčič, 'Yugo-Nostalgia: Cultural Memory and Media in the Former Yugoslavia', *Critical Studies in Media Communication*, vol. 24, no. 1 (2007), pp. 21–38.

[422] Z. Volčič and K. Erjavec, 'The Paradox of Ceca and the Turbo-Folk Audience', *Popular Communication*, vol. 8, no. 2 (2010), pp. 103–19. On Slovenia/Croatia.

[423] A. B. Wachtel, *Making a Nation, Breaking a Nation: Literature and Cultural Politics in Yugoslavia* (Stanford, 1998). On attempts to create common Yugoslav cultures.

[424] I. Žanić, *Flag on the Mountain: A Political Anthropology of War in Croatia and Bosnia*, trans. G. McMaster with C. Hawkesworth (London, 2007). On 'hajduk' mythology.

Index